Collector's
Guide
To

MADE
in
JAPAN

Ceramics

Identification
& Values
# BOOK
# III

Carole Bess White

COLLECTOR BOOKS
A Division of Schroeder Publishing Co., Inc.

The current values of this book should be used only as a guide. They are not intended to set prices, which vary from one section of the country to another. Auction prices as well as dealer prices vary greatly and are affected by condition as well as demand. Neither the Author nor the Publisher assumes responsibility for any losses that might be incurred as a result of consulting this guide.

Searching for a Publisher?

We are always looking for knowledgeable people considered to be experts within their fields. If you feel that there is a real need for a book on your collectible subject and have a large comprehensive collection, contact Collector Books.

On the cover:

Satsuma-style figural ashtray, 4¾" tall, Black Mark #1, $50.00 – 65.00.
Cigarette box with skirtholder lady in multicolored luster glazes, 4¾" long, Red Mark #24, $75.00 – 125.00.
Cigarette set in multicolored luster glazes, tray 7½" wide, all Red Mark #25, $175.00 – 225.00.
Vase in white shiny glaze with multicolored sponged and floral motif, 7½" tall, Red Mark #25, $20.00 – 35.00.
Rabbit powder box in ivory luster glaze, 4" tall, Red Mark #99, $45.00 – 65.00.
Majolica-style basket with floral motif in multicolored shiny glazes, 7" tall, Black Mark #35, $65.00 – 85.00.

Photographs by: Les White
Cover Design: Beth Summers
Book Design: Joyce Cherry

Additional copies of this book may be ordered from:

Collector Books
P.O. Box 3009
Paducah, Kentucky 42002-3009

@ $19.95. Add $2.00 for postage and handling.

Copyright © 1998 by Carole Bess White

CONTENTS

⚐ DEDICATION ⚐

There is one person without whom these books would not be possible—
my wonderful husband and man with a camera!
This book is dedicated to the one I love—LES WHITE

⚐ ACKNOWLEDGMENTS ⚐

Thanks to members of Portland's Rain of Glass Club and all of the collectors and dealers everywhere who shared their knowledge and their collections.

Their generosity resulted in more pictures than this book would hold!

Janice Ahl
Lucille Babcock
Betty Bain
Lizzie, John, Bill, and Nancy Brewer
Shirley Bolman
Lea and Ron Burcham
Carol and Al Carder, Ad Lib, Mult-
    nomah Village, Portland, Oregon
Dave Coons
Richard Cushing
Donna Edgar
Jan Edmonston
Susan Farwell
Jewell Gowan

Mable Hardebeck
Angie Haynes
Lillian Hodges
Gyrid Hyde-Towle
Nirmal Kaur Khalsa
Sewa Singh and Sewa Kaur Khalsa
Grace and Jim Livingston
Louise Meter
Sandy Millius
Marguerite Olds
Floyd Pearson and Skip Schaeffer,
    Cracker Barrel Antiques, Lake-
    head, California
Larry and Trudi Peters

Nancy Ronne, Ph.D.
Neal Skibinski and Michael Kolobaba
Deni Smith
David Spain
Keishi Suzuki
Dan Torres and the late Colleen Bulger
Jim Vanek
W. Joanne Voeller
Jan and Ernie Weaver
Bud Walker

and especially to
Mary Ann and Bob Sloan of Main Street Antique Mall in Toledo, Oregon,
and my two Pats,
Pat and Harold Moyer, Centralia Square Antique Mall, Centralia, Washington,
and Pat Bither, Whistle Stop Antiques, Sherwood, Oregon

Do you collect Made in Japan? Want to have your pieces included in a future publication? Want information on a subscription to the *Made in Japan Info Letter*? Want to order more copies of this book?
Write:
Carole Bess White
P.O. Box 819
Portland, OR 97207
or fax (503) 281-2817 or E-mail CBESSW@aol.com
(No appraisals. Please include SASE for reply.)

 # THE DATA

HISTORY OF MADE IN JAPAN CERAMICS

The United States Customs Bureau enforces the law on marking goods that are imported by America. This law determined how all foreign ceramics exported to the United States were backstamped through the years. As American laws changed, the foreign backstamps were changed to conform to our laws.

1860s – 1891	**JAPONISME ERA** All types of Japanese art and ceramics were eagerly collected in the West. Pieces were marked in Japanese, or not backstamped at all.

1891 – 1921	**NIPPON/HAND PAINTED NIPPON**
	    Before 1891, goods exported to America did not have to be stamped with their country of origin in English. Japanese ceramics usually had no backstamps, or they had artists' or their patrons' names in Japanese characters.
	    The McKinley Tariff, which took effect March 1, 1891, required all imported goods to be stamped in English with their country of origin. At the time, "Nippon" was considered to be an acceptable name for Japan, so most Japanese ceramics of this period were backstamped "Nippon" or "Hand Painted Nippon," often with a company logo as well. However, not all were stamped that way. There were still unmarked pieces, and pieces stamped "Japan" as well.
	    Nippon pieces are priced higher than Made in Japan and are eagerly sought by collectors.

1921 – 1941	**NORITAKE ART DECO** The Noritake Art Deco pieces are considered the "Cadillac" of Made in Japan ceramics by many collectors. They were consistently the best quality and the most beautifully decorated; today they are very avidly collected and priced accordingly!

1921 – 1941	**EARLY MADE IN JAPAN**
	    The U.S. Customs Bureau ruled that "Nippon" was no longer an acceptable synonym. As of August 1, 1921, all goods were supposed to be backstamped "Japan."
	    Technically, the MIJ era began when the Nippon era ended in 1921, but it really was not that precise. At some point the U.S. Customs Bureau may have required that the words "Made In" be added to the backstamps, but this was not always done. Unmarked pieces sometimes slipped through Customs, but most of the ceramics from 1921 to 1941 are marked either "Japan" or "Made in Japan."
	    Sometimes, all pieces in a set are not backstamped. The profit margin on ceramics was slim, and a factory could save a little labor cost by not marking every piece in a set. If pieces in a set have different backstamps, it is because there often was not room for "Made in Japan," or a company logo, so they just used "Japan" on some of the smaller pieces.
	    Early Made in Japan pieces, especially Art Deco and lusters, have come into their own and are very collectible.

1947 – 1952	**OCCUPIED JAPAN/MADE IN OCCUPIED JAPAN**
	    When America and Japan went to war in 1941, trade ceased, so no new shipments of Made in Japan were imported. However, pieces already in this country continued to sell. After the war, the United States occupied Japan from September 2, 1945, until April 28, 1952. The Occupied Japan backstamp era truly began August 15, 1947, when Japanese ceramics companies again were allowed to engage in private foreign trade.
	    The U.S. Customs Bureau decreed in 1949 that Japanese goods could be marked "Occupied Japan," "Made in Occupied Japan," "Japan," or "Made in Japan." Again, some were not marked at all.
	    Occupied ware has its ardent collectors as well, but prices seem to be about equal to or, in some cases, lower than early Made in Japan.

1952 – TODAY	**POST-WAR MADE IN JAPAN**
	    When the occupation ended in 1952, marks no longer contained the word "Occupied," so pieces were again marked only with "Japan" or "Made in Japan."
	    This is when the paper label era really began. Prior to WW II, paper labels were flimsy and the glue was often not strong, so the Customs Bureau usually made importers replace the labels with indelible ink backstamps. In the fifties, technology improved and paper labels were allowed.
	    The two most common types of labels seem to be, small oval or rectangular blue or black paper with white letters; two-color metallic, such as black or red, with gold or silver lettering. The real sleepers are the post-WW II Made in Japan pieces because they are still very affordable!

Japanese ceramic exporting began less than 150 years ago. Before then, Japan was a closed country and traded with the West only through a Dutch company. In 1853, the United States government sent Commodore Perry to open diplomatic and trade relations with Japan, and by the 1860s, Japan was trading with the West.

The Japonisme Era lasted from the 1860s until 1891. Japanese art and ceramics were avidly collected in America and Europe, and Western painters and ceramic artists were greatly influenced by Japanese designs. During this period, Japanese ceramics were either marked in Japanese, or not marked at all.

During the Nippon Era, Japan began manufacturing and exporting more commercial types of ceramics, including Western style dishes and novelties. (Japanese manufacturers refer to almost everything that is not a dish as a novelty.) At first, Japanese ceramics producers copied German originals, but as time went on, techniques became more sophisticated, and some ceramics equaled or surpassed Germany's in quality and workmanship. (See Plates 284 and 285 for an illustration of this point.)

German "original" cat bookends, marked Germany, 4¾" tall, $45.00 – 65.00.

German "original" incense burner, 4" tall, no mark, $50.00 – 75.00.

German "original" cigarette jar and ashtray set, donkey 4" tall, ashtrays all marked Germany, holder no mark, $45.00 – 65.00.

During World War I, Germany could not trade with America, which created an opportunity for Japan to expand their ceramic exports. Another opportunity came when the American stock market crashed on October 29, 1929. Economic conditions in America were grim during the Great Depression, but the desire for cheap, colorful, and attractive Japanese novelties and dishes grew. The golden years of Made in Japan lasted until about 1939. Ceramics from the Orient were very popular, and the largest number of what many collectors today consider to be the most creative, interesting, and desirable collectibles were made during this time.

Among the most desirable of all ceramics from the Made in Japan Era are those from the Noritake Company, Ltd. Noritake pieces are almost always superior in quality and design. The Art Deco pieces are especially popular, but the Noritake backstamp usually fetches a higher price than comparable pieces from other factories.

By 1939, Made in Japan ceramics were no longer the fad item they once were, but we still bought a respectable amount of them right up until we declared war on Japan in 1941. During the war, and even for some years after, many Americans destroyed their Made in Japan ceramics, or obscured the backstamps on pieces they wanted to keep. Not all Americans felt that way, and some stores that had pre-World War II stock of Made in Japan ceramics continued to sell them throughout the war.

After World War II, American forces occupied Japan. During the Occupation, Japan needed industries that would rebuild their economy and allow restitution. The ceramics industry was approved by SCAP (Supreme Commander, Allied Powers) because it met these criteria while not allowing rearmament. Of course, new ceramic designs were created, but also during this time the Japanese did imitate or recreate the same types of novelties that were successful before World War II.

This creates a tremendous challenge for collectors today, because it is virtually impossible to say for 100% sure whether a piece was made before or after World War II. There is always the possibility that pieces that look and feel like pre-World War II, and even those pictured in older catalogs, might have been made during the occupation.

Also, molds that survived the war were re-used any time the manufacturer got an order for those pieces. A good example of this is the elephant mug in Plate 550 of this book, one of a set of six which Les and I purchased brand new in 1969 at Import Plaza in Portland, Oregon, long before we ever thought of collecting and studying Made in Japan ceramics. They came in cobalt blue or forest green glaze, and they had paper labels, which of course washed right off because I was young and ignorant and actually wanted to use the mugs! In Book 2 of *The Collector's Guide to Made in Japan Ceramics*, the same mug blank glazed in multicolored lusters is shown in Plate 565, and there it definitely looks pre-World War II.

Today, the ceramics industry in Japan is winding down. Most of the Japanese ceramics companies have closed entirely or moved to other countries where labor is cheaper. This means that any records that might have survived the war are now lost or destroyed, and workers have scattered. Thank goodness Noritake is still in business, as is Mikasa, but Japan's main exports are cars and electronics, not pottery.

During its heyday, Japan exported more than 750,000 tableware patterns to the United States, and probably close to that number of novelties.

⊿ DATING MADE IN JAPAN PIECES ⊾

Collectors of fine Japanese ceramics refer to Japanese historical periods when discussing periods of production. These periods are based on the years of the current Emperor's reign. The Made in Japan Era includes:

NAME OF PERIOD	EMPEROR	YEARS
MEIJI PERIOD	MUTSUHITO	1867 – 1912
TAISHO PERIOD	YOSHIHITO	1912 – 1926
SHOWA PERIOD	HIROHITO	1926 – 1989

Dating pieces can be the biggest challenge to collectors, even bigger than value! For some reason, it matters terribly to some of us to know exactly where, when, and by whom our piece was made. As we advance in our personal collecting journeys, we may somewhat grow away from these concerns. If we like a piece, we come to realize that it's not critically important if it was made in Tokyo in 1932 or Nagoya in 1938. And this is a good thing, because most of this information is just not available to us.

However, the good news is that there is one concrete piece of information we can access—patent numbers. The bad news is that not very many ceramic pieces have patent numbers on the backstamps.

Patent numbers simply show the first year that a patent was issued. The piece could have been made any time after then. However, patent numbers remain active in most countries for 15 years or so unless extensions are granted, so they can give you a pretty good ballpark time period.

JAPANESE UTILITY, DESIGN, AND TRADEMARK NUMBERS

Japan began granting patent numbers in 1885, and there are four categories:

PATENT	UTILITY	DESIGN	TRADEMARK
includes invented objects and devices	includes improvements to inventions that have already been patented	applies to the visual appearance of the object, such as shape, color, and pattern	includes logos, symbols, characters or letters that apply to a company or object
A common example of Patent vs. Utility numbering would be the VCR. The invention of the VCR was granted a patent number, and subsequent improvements are given Utility numbers. If you look inside your VCR, you should see one Patent number and several Utility numbers.		Examples of Design patents would be fabrics, wallpapers, and, of course, china patterns.	Trademarks may be color specific, so two companies could trademark the identical logo art, such as a dragon's head, in two different colors.

YEAR	UTILITY	DESIGN	TRADEMARK
1889	-	1	1
1890	-	23	2920
1895	-	393	6169
1900	-	834	13822
1905	1	2281	23384
1910	16072	5579	39575
1915	34225	11165	70875
1920	51222	17763	112025
1925	75387	24590	161059
1930	128434	45778	215483
1935	194928	69287	274925
1940	269853	92608	355145
1945	343723	100432	403881
1950	358040	104192	426420
1955	411395	128189	516583
1960	494051	182881	622841
1965	634802	256909	750511
1970	772386	337673	936967
1975	946266	449159	1276227
1980	1193280	624960	1735643
1985	1462284	786965	2185702
1990	1683285	961265	2779671

If the backstamp does not include "PAT" or "PATENT NUMBER" in the wording, then how does the collector know what the number is? When inventors come up with a new, original object or device, they can apply for and be granted a Patent number. If it is in some way improved upon, a Utility patent can be applied for to protect the improvement. The original patent number still applies and is now accompanied by a utility number, although only one number may be shown on the piece. The numbers we are most likely to find on ceramic items will be a Patent number for an object with a distinct purpose, and a Design number where the object is common but the design distinct.

The distinction of color in trademarks explains why it is not illegal in the Japanese system to copy the Noritake trademark of the "M"-in-wreath in a color not trademarked by the Noritake Company. Similarly, the sharp attention to detail in a pictograph-based language such as Japanese explains why other companies can legally make very close copies of the Noritake trademark, for instance the Noritake Mark with the wreath upside down. Close copies are accepted in countries that use a pictograph-based language, whereas the same close copy would be deemed an infringement in a country such as the United States where the language is based on a character alphabet. For more information on Japanese Patent numbers, write:

Information Desk (Gaikoku-sodan)
Internal Affairs Division
Japanese Patent Office (Tokkyocho)
3-4-3 Kasumigaseki Chiyoda-ku
Tokyo 100, Japan
Japanese Patent numbers & information Copyright R. Cushing, reprinted by permission.

JAPANESE PATENT NUMBERS 1885 — 1990

YEAR	NUMBER	YEAR	NUMBER	YEAR	NUMBER	YEAR	NUMBER
1885	1	1912	21035	1939	114314	1966	366711
1886	100	1913	22809	1940	120227	1967	393026
1887	305	1914	24830	1941	126943	1968	413799
1888	414	1915	26654	1942	133629	1969	441771
1889	597	1916	28436	1943	141606	1970	469428
1890	807	1917	30233	1944	147988	1971	500307
1891	1046	1918	31681	1945	156324	1972	536754
1892	1413	1919	33334	1946	158664	1973	578208
1893	1792	1920	35349	1947	161068	1974	620536
1894	2110	1921	37510	1948	162124	1975	660162
1895	2436	1922	41103	1949	164009	1976	706890
1896	2664	1923	44107	1950	167949	1977	747207
1897	2833	1924	46238	1951	172221	1978	799815
1898	3021	1925	48165	1952	178490	1979	845319
1899	3314	1926	53254	1953	183976	1980	889423
1900	3610	1927	56774	1954	189782	1981	935529
1901	4197	1928	61145	1955	196852	1982	986433
1902	4803	1929	65849	1956	205409	1983	1037034
1903	5674	1930	70939	1957	214839	1984	1091735
1904	6878	1931	75915	1958	224652	1985	1153535
1905	8131	1932	80233	1959	234624	1986	1203635
1906	9385	1933	85079	1960	244902	1987	1263535
1907	11029	1934	90581	1961	256154	1988	1325935
1908	13071	1935	95254	1962	277100	1989	1381235
1909	15126	1936	100020	1963	292803	1990	1444536
1910	16994	1937	104856	1964	316106		
1911	18763	1938	109472	1965	339804		

U.S. PATENT NUMBERS

YEAR	NUMBER	YEAR	NUMBER	YEAR	NUMBER
1850	6,981	1900	640,167	1950	2,492,944
1855	12,601	1905	778,834	1955	2,698,414
1860	25,279	1910	945,010	1960	2,919,441
1865	48,969	1915	1,128,212	1965	3,163,865
1870	98,471	1920	1,326,899	1970	3,487,470
1875	158,350	1925	1,521,590	1975	3,858,241
1880	232,978	1930	1,742,181	1980	4,180,867
1885	310,163	1935	1,985,878	1985	4,490,855
1890	418,665	1940	2,185,170	1990	4,890,335
1895	531,619	1945	2,366,154		

THE MARKS

There were THOUSANDS of different marks used on Made in Japan ceramics over the years. Japanese manufacturers, exporters, importers, and American retail sellers could mark pieces however they preferred, as long as they contained the words "Japan" or "Made in Japan."

Because of the huge number of marks and labels, we show only those on pieces in this book, and in Books 1 and 2. If your piece has a different mark than one shown here, that does not necessarily make it rare because it's not "in the book."

HOT NEWS FLASH!! THE CHIKARAMACHI MARK, FORMERLY UNKNOWN, HAS BEEN OFFICIALLY IDENTIFIED AS A NORITAKE MARK! MARK #36 DATES FROM 1928.

The CHIKARAMACHI backstamp was created when all the painting factories of Morimura Gumi (Noritake) in Japan were united as Kin-yo Gumi at Chikara-machi and Shumoku-cho in Nagoya. The first version of the CHIKARAMACHI Mark dates from 1912, and there are two other versions dating from 1928.

(Source: Noritake, *History of the Materials Development and Chronology of Backstamps*, May 1997, Noritake Company Ltd., courtesy of Mr. Keishi Suzuki and David Spain.)

MARKS 1–4, 40 NO SPECIFIC COMPANY—NEARLY ALL COMPANIES USED VARIATIONS OF THESE MARKS AT ONE TIME OR ANOTHER	**MARK 57** UNITED CHINA & GIFT CO. (FORMERLY UNITED CHINA & GLASS CO.), STILL IN BUSINESS
MARKS 5–9, 13–19, 22, 23A, 27, 29, 33–34 37–39, 41, 46, 50–52, 55–56, 62–62A, 66–67, 72–74, 76–98, 100–103, 105–110, 112–140 UNKNOWN	**MARK 58, 58a** NAGOYA BOEKI SHOKAI, STILL IN BUSINESS
MARK 10 SHOFU INDUSTRIAL CO., LTD., IN BUSINESS BEFORE WWII, CLOSED SEPTEMBER 1965	**MARK 59** NANRI BOEKI & CO., CLOSED 1978
MARKS 11, 12, 21, 21a, 21b, 32, 43, 43a, 44 TASHIRO SHOTEN LTD., IN BUSINESS BEFORE WWII, CLOSED 1954	**MARKS 60, 60a, 61** MOGI SHOJI & CO., STILL IN BUSINESS
MARKS 20, 24, 25, 30, 30A SEIEI & CO., IN BUSINESS BEFORE WWII, CLOSED 1962. (Mark 30A was registered in 1932.)	**MARK 63** YOKOI SEI-ICHI SHOTEN, CLOSED 1942
MARK 23 NIHON YOKO BOEKI CO., STILL IN BUSINESS	**MARK 64, 75** NAGOYA SEITO SHO (MARK 64) STARTED BUSINESS C1908, WAS PURCHASED BY SUMIMOTO STEEL INDUSTRY COMPANY C. WORLD WAR II AND THE NAME WAS CHANGED TO NARUMI SEITO SHO (MARK 75 WAS REGISTERED IN 1934). NARUMI IS STILL IN BUSINESS.
MARKS 26, 36, 53, 53a, 53b, 54 NIPPON TOKI KASHA (NORITAKE CO., LIMITED) FOUNDED 1876 – STILL IN BUSINESS. MARK #26 DATES FROM 1924; #36 FROM 1928; #53 FROM 1915; #53A FROM 1908.	**MARK 65** YAMASHIRO RYUHEI (LATER CHANGED TO MARUYAMA TOKI), OPENED IN 1914, STOPPED PRODUCTION 1989
MARK 28 HOTTA YU SHOTEN & CO., IN BUSINESS BEFORE WWII, CLOSED 1947	**MARK 68** IWATA (COULD BE NAME OF MANUFACTURER OR EXPORTER), CLOSING DATE UNKNOWN
MARK 31 MARUKA TAJIMI BOEKI SHOKAI, STILL IN BUSINESS	**MARKS 69 & 70** MANUFACTURED IN JAPAN FOR THE AMERICAN COMPANY, JOSEF ORIGINALS, FROM 1955 THROUGH THE EARLY 1970'S
MARK 42 ENESCO, JAPAN, CLOSED NOVEMBER 1978	**MARK 71** AICHI TOKI SHOKAI (FORMERLY HIGO HOTEN), STILL IN BUSINESS
MARK 45 HANAI GIRYO CO., IN BUSINESS BEFORE WWII, CLOSING DATE UNKNOWN	**MARK 99** SHIMIZU-ROKUNOSUKO SHOTEN, NAGOYA, REGISTERED THIS MARK IN 1932. THEY CLOSED BEFORE WORLD WAR II.
MARKS 47 & 48 TSUJISO TOKI CO. IN BOOK 1, MARK #44 WAS SUBSTITUTED FOR MARK #48. MARK #48 IS CORRECT IN THIS BOOK AND BOOK 2.	**MARK 104** MARUGO SEITO SHO INC., TOKONAME CITY, AICHI PREFECTURE, REGISTERED THIS MARK IN 1950. THEY STOPPED PRODUCTION IN THE 1980S.
MARK 49 KINKOZAN, 1645 – 1927	**MARKS 111, 111A** EMPIRE TRADING CO., LTD., NAGOYA, WHICH HAD NO FACTORY, REGISTERED THESE MARKS IN 1950. THEY CLOSED THEIR BUSINESS IN THE 1980S.

"TOKI" is Japanese for chinaware or pottery, and "KAISHA" is company.

Mark 1

Mark 2

Mark 3

Mark 3A

Mark 4

Mark 5

Mark 6

Mark 7

Mark 8

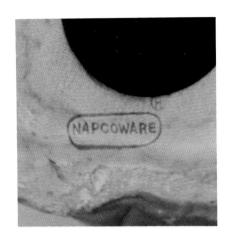

Mark 8A

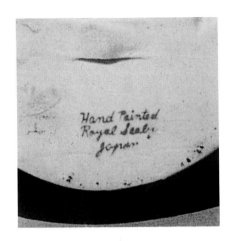

Mark 9

Mark 10

Mark 11

Mark 12

Mark 12A

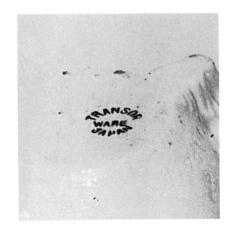

Mark 13

Mark 14

Mark 15

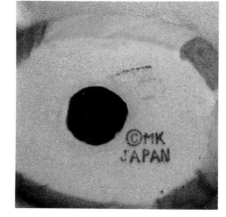

Mark 16

Mark 17

Mark 18

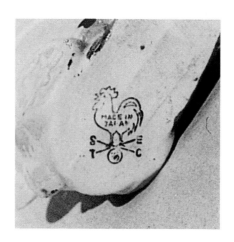

Mark 19

Mark 20

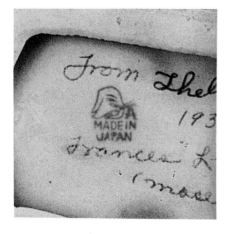

Mark 21

Mark 21A

Mark 21B

Mark 22

Mark 23

Mark 23A

Mark 23B

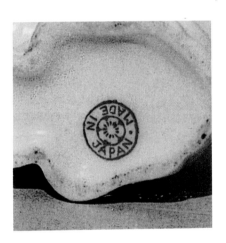

Mark 24

Mark 25

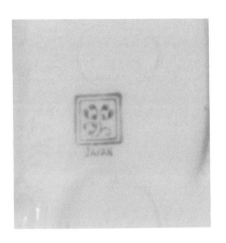

Mark 26

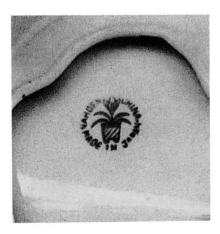

Mark 27

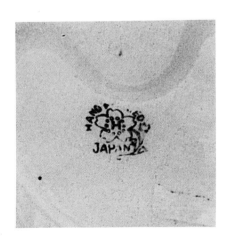

Mark 28

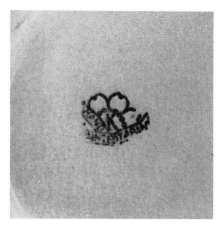

Mark 29

Mark 30

Mark 30A

Mark 31

Mark 32

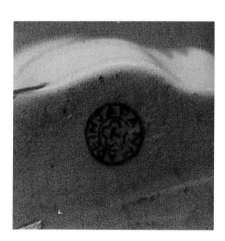

Mark 32A

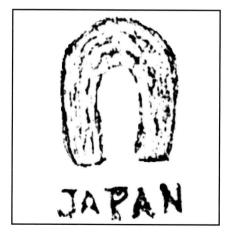

Mark 33

Mark 34

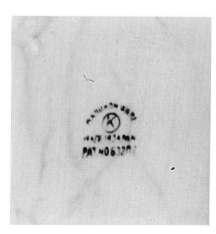

Mark 35

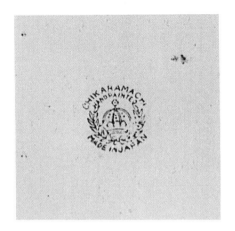

Mark 36

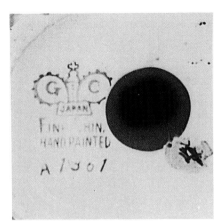

Mark 37

Mark 38

Mark 38A

Mark 39

Mark 40

Mark 41

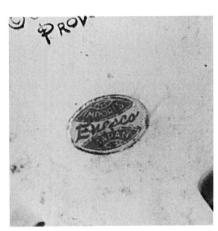

Mark 42

Mark 43

Mark 43A

Mark 44

Mark 45

Mark 46

Mark 47

Mark 48

Mark 49

Mark 50

Mark 51

Mark 51A

Mark 52

Mark 53

Mark 53A

Mark 53B

Mark 54

Mark 55

Mark 56

Mark 57

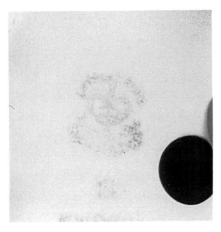

Mark 58

Mark 58A

Mark 59

Mark 60

Mark 60A

Mark 61

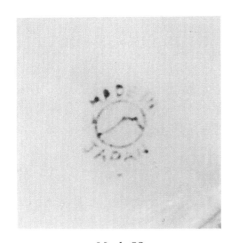

Mark 62

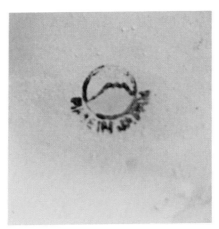

Mark 62A

Mark 63

Mark 64

Mark 64A

Mark 65

Mark 66

Mark 66A

Mark 66B

Mark 66C

Mark 66D

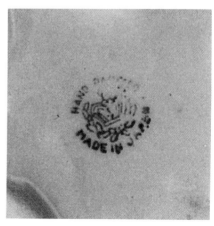

Mark 67

Mark 68

Mark 69

Mark 70

Mark 71

Mark 72

Mark 73

Mark 73A

Mark 74

Mark 75

Mark 76

Mark 77

Mark 78

Mark 79

Mark 79A

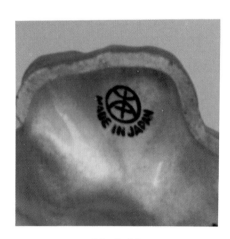

Mark 80

Mark 81

Mark 81(close-up)

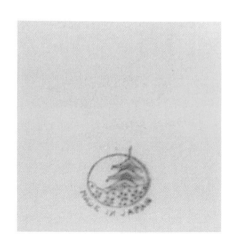

Mark 82

Mark 83

Mark 84

Mark 85

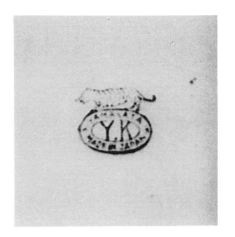

Mark 86

Mark 87

Mark 88

Mark 89

Mark 90

Mark 91

Mark 92

Mark 93

Mark 94

Mark 95

Mark 95A

Mark 96

Mark 97

Mark 98

Mark 99

Mark 100

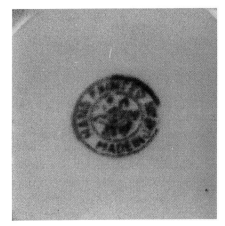

Mark 101

Mark 102

Mark 103

Mark 104

Mark 105

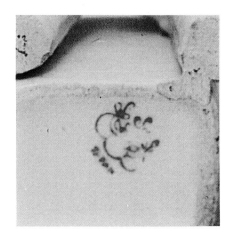

Mark 106

Mark 107

Mark 108

Mark 109

Mark 110

Mark 111

Mark 111A

Mark 112

Mark 112A

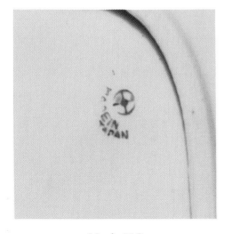

Mark 113

Mark 114

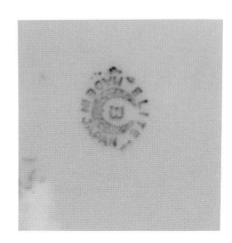

Mark 115

Mark 116

Mark 117

Mark 118

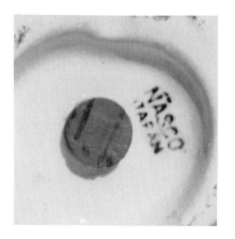

Mark 119

Mark 120

Mark 121

Mark 122

Mark 123

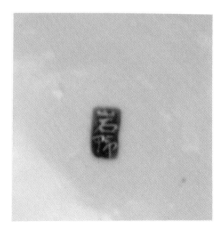

Mark 124

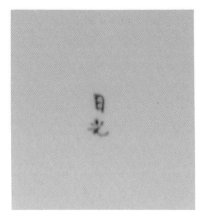

Mark 125

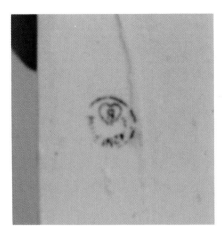

Mark 126

Mark 127

Mark 128

Mark 129

Mark 130

Mark 131

Mark 132

Mark 133

Mark 134

Mark 135

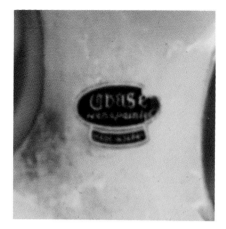

Mark 136

Mark 137

Mark 138

Mark 139

Mark 140

≥⊿ THE COLLECTIBLES ⊿≤

Measurements are rounded off to the nearest quarter-inch. Even though the ink color of the backstamps is not an indication of age, it is included where possible.

The naming of pieces' functions is based on research and direct knowledge, or comparison with similar objects. However, what the actual function was meant to be is often lost to us today. Items were sold with multiple functions, depending on what was popular with consumers at the time, or with no function at all. So my mayonnaise set might be a sauce dish to you and a whipped cream set to your grandmother. Since there are no "function police" to arrest us for misnaming, we'll just have to agree that if it's our piece, we can call it whatever we darn well please!

Some items are noted as Akiyama pieces. The Akiyama family had Oriental gift stores in Portland, Oregon, from the 1920s until 1942. They were interned for the duration of World War II, so they stored the remaining stock in the basement of their house. It stayed there until 1987, when Hanji Akiyama, their son, sold the house and placed the pieces in a local antique mall.

Other pieces are noted as shown in the Sears & Roebuck, Larkin, or Butler Brothers catalogs. Luckily, a few pieces have been in their owners' families since before World War II; these are so noted.

The main types of glazes used on Made in Japan ceramics are luster (metallic or pearly overglaze); shiny (glossy); matte (flat, opaque with no shine); semi-matte (opaque with some shine); crackle (glaze that is designed to have a crackled surface). Bisque pieces usually have cold paint on them, but sometimes they have fired glazes.

Prices are shown in ranges to reflect the lower and higher-priced regions of the country.

This book, along with Volumes 1 and 2, gives an overview of as many types as possible of the thousands of Made in Japan ceramic collectibles made over the years.

◿ ART DECO ◺

Art Deco was the prevailing style of the 1920s through the 1940s. Derived from natural and geometric forms, Art Deco pieces can have overall patterns of flowers, fruits, figures, or geometric forms, or they may have panels with Deco motifs. Sometimes the shape of the piece itself may be Art Deco.

Plate 1. Ashtray with butler figure, in multicolored shiny glazes, 4¾", Black Mark #1, $25.00 – 45.00.

Plate 2. Club card suit ashtray with clown figure, multicolored luster glazes, 4" wide, Red Mark #1, $50.00 – 75.00.

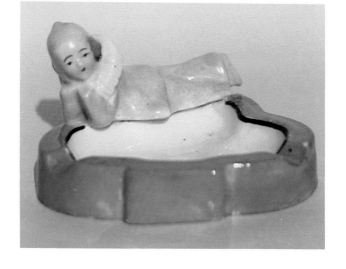

Plate 3. Club card suit ashtray in blue and multicolored shiny glazes, 4" wide, Blind Mark #1, $50.00 – 75.00.

Plate 4. Ashtray with attached cigarette holder in tan luster glaze with black trim and multicolored lady with fan motif, 4¼" wide, Black Mark #1, $50.00 – 75.00.

Plate 5. Ashtray with hands clasping a matchholder in multicolored luster glazes *(pictured in a 1920s Butler Brothers catalog as a "Cigar rest & holder" as part of an assortment of one dozen different pieces for $4.00 per dozen)*, 5" tall, Red Mark #12, $45.00 – 65.00.

Plate 6. Cat ashtray with snuffers in yellow and multicolored luster glazes, 2¼" tall, Red Mark #1 and Blind Mark #1, $15.00 – 25.00.

Plate 7. Footed basket in teal and multicolored luster and shiny glazes, 5½" tall, Black Mark #1, $20.00 – 30.00.

Plate 9. Noritake one-handled bowl in multicolored luster and shiny glazes with white house motif, 6" wide, Red Mark #53, $35.00 – 65.00.

Plate 8. Noritake basket-handled bowl, tan luster glaze with multicolored fruit motif, 8½" wide, Blue Mark #26, $65.00 – 95.00.

Plate 10. Noritake lug-handled bowl in teal luster glaze with multicolored house motif, 6" wide, Green Mark #53, $25.00 – 55.00.

Plate 11. Bowl with Tudor house motif in multicolored shiny glazes, 7" wide, Red Mark #2, $40.00 – 60.00.

Plate 12. Noritake bowl in multicolored luster glazes, with white house motif, 8" wide, Blue Mark #26, $65.00 – 85.00.

Plate 13. Noritake handled bowl with house in yellow and multicolored shiny glazes, 8" wide, Green Mark #53, $65.00-85.00.

Plate 14. Noritake footed bowl in multicolored luster glazes, 6" wide, Red Mark #53, $45.00 – 75.00.

Plate 15. Noritake footed bowl in multicolored luster glazes, 6" wide, Red Mark #53, $45.00 – 75.00.

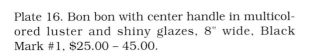

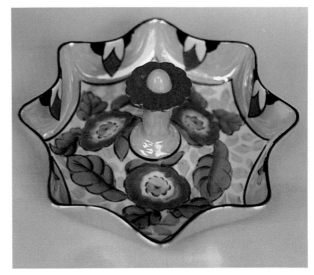

Plate 16. Bon bon with center handle in multicolored luster and shiny glazes, 8" wide, Black Mark #1, $25.00 – 45.00.

Plate 17. Noritake cake plate with floral motif in multicolored luster glazes, 9½" wide, Blue Mark #25, $35.00 – 55.00.

Plate 18. Children's dish set in pink shiny glaze with multicolored floral motif *(the shapes are very Deco, but the motif is more Majolica-style, so the set could have gone in either category)*, teapot 4½" tall, all Black Mark #1, $30.00 – 55.00 as pictured, ($125.00 – 225.00 if complete with 4 or 6 cups, saucers, and plates).

Plate 19. Chocolate set in blue and tan luster glazes with multicolored bird & floral motif, pot 8¼" tall, Red Mark #52, $68.00 – 78.00 as pictured ($135.00 – 165.00 complete with 4 or 6 cups and saucers).

Some collectors call these "compotes" but others call them "comports," which is a shortened form of *comportiere.* Think of it this way: we use comports to hold or carry our compote!

Plate 20. Noritake handled comport in multicolored luster glazes with white house motif, 10" wide, Red Mark #26, $60.00 – 75.00.

Plate 21. Noritake comport with floral motif in multicolored luster and shiny glazes, 2¾" tall, Green Mark #53, $45.00 – 65.00.

Plate 22. Handled comport with floral motif in multicolored luster and shiny glazes, 6¾" wide, no Mark, $35.00 – 55.00.

Plate 23. Condiment set with floral motif in multicolored luster and shiny glazes, 7¾ wide, bottle no Mark, tray, salt and pepper Black Mark #1, $30.00 – 65.00.

Plate 24. Condiment set with floral motif in multicolored luster and shiny glazes, 7" wide, tray and mustard pot Red Mark #28, salt and pepper Red Mark #1, $30.00 – 65.00.

Plate 25. Cream and sugar on tray in teal and multicolored luster glazes, tray 7" wide, all Black Mark #1, $55.00 – 96.00.

Plate 27. Cream and sugar on tray in cream, amber and multicolored luster glazes, tray 6½" wide, all Red Mark #1, $55.00 – 96.00.

Plate 26. Goldcastle cream and sugar on tray in multicolored luster glazes with floral decals, tray 5¼" tall, all Green Mark #43, $55.00 – 96.00.

Plate 28. Cream and sugar with dot motif in multicolored luster glazes *(shown in the 1929 Sears catalog with a different motif for 89¢ per pair)*, creamer 3" tall, all Red Mark #20, $35.00 – 55.00.

Plate 29. Sailboat lamp in white shiny glaze, 6¾" to top of ceramic post, Red Mark #25, $25.00 – 35.00.

Plate 30. Noritake lemon plate in multicolored luster glazes with white house motif, 5¼" wide, Red Mark #53, $45.00 – 75.00.

Plate 31. Noritake lemon plate in green and multicolored shiny glazes, 5¾" wide, Red Mark #53, $45.00 – 55.00.

Plate 32. Noritake lemon plate in blue and multicolored luster glazes with red floral motif, 5¾" wide, Red Mark #53, $45.00 – 55.00.

Plate 33. Noritake lemon plate with floral motif and blue triangle band in multicolored luster and shiny glazes, 5½" wide, Red Mark #53, $45.00 – 55.00.

Plate 34. Noritake lemon plate in blue luster glaze with orange and blue floral motif, 5½" wide, Red Mark #53, $45.00 – 55.00.

Plate 35. Match holder with two gentlemen in multicolored shiny glazes, 4½" tall, Red Mark #32, $75.00 – 125.00.

Plate 36. Noritake muffineer (or berry sugar and cream or waffle sugar and syrup—they were advertised as all three at different times) set in multicolored shiny glazes, 6¾" tall, Red Mark #53, $65.00 – 95.00.

Plate 37. Muffineer or berry sugar and cream set in multicolored luster glaze, 6" tall, Red Mark #20, $65.00 – 95.00.

Plate 38. Muffineer or berry sugar and cream set in orange and multicolored matte glazes, 5¾" tall, Red Mark #24, $65.00 – 95.00.

Plate 39. Noritake napkin ring set in multicolored luster glazes *(shown in a 1920s catalog for $1 per set "with premium"),* 1¾" tall, Red Mark #53, set $100.00 – 150.00.

Plate 40. Tall pitcher in multicolored shiny glazes, may have come with a lid, 7¾" tall, Black Mark #1, $45.00 – 75.00.

Plate 41. (Left) Planter in cream and multicolored shiny glazes, 4¼" tall, Black Mark #1, $20.00 – 30.00 (Right) Cache pot and plate in green and cream shiny glaze, 3¼" tall, all Black Mark #1, $20.00 – 30.00.

Plate 42. Noritake salad set with teal luster glaze and multicolored lobster motif, 11¾" wide, platter no Mark, pitcher Red Mark #26, $85.00 – 105.00 as pictured ($125.00 – 175.00 if complete with matching serving spoons).

Plate 43. Salt and pepper in blue and tan luster glaze with multicolored bird motif (*shown in the 1928 Sears catalog with a different motif for 45¢ a pair*), 4¼" tall, Red Mark #1, $22.00 – 37.00.

Plate 44. Sandwich server in teal, blue, and multicolored luster glazes with floral motif, 10" wide, Red Mark #26, $45.00 – 75.00.

Plate 45. Sandwich server in tan, lavender, and multicolored luster glazes with floral motif, 10" wide, Red Mark #26, $45.00 – 75.00.

Plate 46. Stacking teapot set with tile in cream and multicolored shiny glazes, tile 5" wide, Red Mark 21B, $68.00 – 78.00.

Plate 47. (Left) Goldcastle teapot in yellow and multicolored luster glazes, 6½" tall, Red Mark #43, $35.00 – 50.00. (Right) Teapot in aqua and multicolored luster glazes, 7¼" tall, Black Mark #1, $35.00 – 50.00.

Plate 48. Teapot in cobalt blue and multicolored shiny glazes, 6" tall, Blind Mark #1, $30.00 – 45.00.

Plate 49. Teapot in blue and tan luster glaze with multicolored floral motif *(shown in the 1933 Sears catalog with assorted colors and decorations for 49¢ each),* 6½" tall, Black Mark #1, $35.00 – 50.00.

Plate 50. Teapot in white shiny glaze with gold luster trim, 4½" tall, Black and Red Mark #64A, $35.00 – 50.00.

Plate 51. Teapot with house motif in multicolored luster glazes, 7" tall, Red Mark #1, $35.00 – 50.00.

Plate 52. Noritake tray in multicolored luster glazes with floral motif, 9½" wide, Red Mark #26, $50.00 – 65.00.

Plate 53. Goldcastle square vase in multicolored luster glazes, 7" tall, Black Mark #43, $50.00 – 75.00.

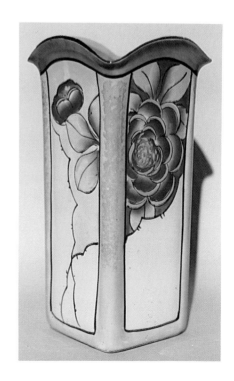

Plate 54. Fan-shaped vase in multicolored luster glazes *(pictured in a 1920s Butler Brothers catalog as part of an assortment of one dozen different pieces for $4.00 per dozen)*, 7" tall, Red Mark #12, $50.00 – 75.00.

Plate 55. Vase in tan luster glaze with multicolored floral motif *(shown in the 1932 Sears catalog for 89¢ each)*, 7" tall, Red Mark #32, $50.00 – 75.00.

Plate 56. Vase with multicolored floral motif *(pictured in a 1920s Butler Brothers catalog as part of an assortment of one dozen different pieces for $4.00 per dozen)*, 6¾" tall, Red Mark #12, $50.00 – 75.00.

Plate 57. Noritake vase in multicolored luster glazes with red floral motif (the same blank as the vase in Plate 272 of *The Collector's Guide to Made in Japan Ceramics, Book 1*, which has the Goldcastle Mark #43, not the Noritake Mark), 8½" tall, Red Mark #26, $75.00 – 100.00.

Plate 58. Vase in cream luster glaze with multicolored floral motif, 6¾" tall, Red Mark #12A, $50.00 – 75.00.

Plate 59. Vase in blue luster glaze with multicolored floral motif, 6½" tall, Red Mark #11, $50.00 – 75.00.

Plate 60. Vase with handles in cream luster glaze with multicolored floral motif, 7½" tall, Red Mark #12A, $50.00 – 75.00.

Plate 61. Vase in cream luster glaze with multi-colored floral motif, 7½" tall, Red Mark #12A, $50.00 – 75.00.

Plate 62. Triangular vase in multicolored luster and shiny glazes, 7" tall, $50.00 – 75.00.

Plate 63. Noritake swan vase in multicolored luster glazes, 4½" tall, Red Mark #26, $75.00 – 125.00.

Plate 64. Vase in pink shiny glaze, 5" tall, Black Mark #1, $25.00 – 40.00.

Plate 65. Vase with dog in maroon shiny glaze, 6¼" tall, Black Mark #1, $25.00 – 40.00.

Plate 66. Tri-part vase in blue shiny glaze, 7¾" tall, Black Mark #1, $20.00 – 35.00.

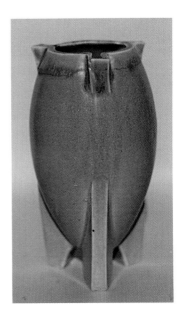

Plate 67. Vase in blue and brown semi-matte glaze, 5¾" tall, Black Mark #1, $25.00 – 40.00.

Plate 68. Handled vase in blue shiny glaze, 5¾" tall, Black Mark #1, $25.00 – 40.00.

Plate 69. (Left) Vase with tulips and sprigged on insect handles in blue semi-matte glaze, 8" tall, Black Mark #1, $50.00 – 75.00. (Right) Vase with multi-colored floral motif after the style of Clarice Cliff, 9" tall, Red Mark #25, $75.00 – 100.00.

Plate 70. Lady head wall hangings in multicolored shiny glazes, 4½" tall, Black Mark #1, $30.00 – 40.00 each.

Plate 71. Goldcastle lady head wall hangings in multicolored shiny glaze, 6¾" tall, Blue Mark #43 and Blind Mark #65, $50.00 – 75.00 each.

Plate 72. Wall pocket in aqua shiny glaze, 7" tall, Black Mark #1, $50.00 – 85.00.

This set is at the end of the Art Deco section because, while the motif has elements of Art Deco and the pieces reflect a definite 1920s style in their colors and shapes, the motif also has elements of Art Nouveau, so it is not as strong as most other Art Deco patterns in the traditional sense of the word. We affectionately refer to it as "Purple Haze," which is, of course, NOT a factory name! *(The motif was described in the 1927 Sears Catalog as a "scenic medallion.")*

Plate 73. Noritake low handled bowl, 8½" wide, Green Mark #53, $45.00 – 65.00.

Plate 74. Noritake salad or serving bowl, 10" wide, Green Mark #53, $45.00 – 65.00.

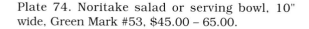

❧ BELLS ❧

Plate 106. Colonial lady bell in multi-colored shiny glazes, 3½" tall, Black Mark #2, $12.00 – 20.00.

Plate 107. Colonial lady bell in multicolored shiny glazes with label SOUVENIR OF RACINE, the mate to the bell in Plate 461C in *The Collector's Guide to Made in Japan Ceramics*, *Book 1*, 3" tall, Red Mark #2, $20.00 – 35.00.

Plate 108. Lady bell in multicolored shiny glazes, 4¾" tall, Black Mark #1, $12.00 – 20.00.

❧ BISCUIT BARRELS ❧

Plate 109. Tiny biscuit barrel in multicolored luster and shiny glazes, 4" tall, Red Mark #1, $15.00 – 25.00.

Plate 110. (Left) Biscuit or sugar barrel in orange and white shiny glaze, 6¼" tall, Red Mark #11, $48.00 – 68.00. (Right) Biscuit barrel in green shiny glaze with blown-out motif, 8" tall, Blind Mark #88, $48.00 – 68.00.

Plate 111. (Left) Pineapple-textured biscuit barrel in white shiny glaze with pink and green floral motif, 7" tall, Black Mark #1, $48.00 – 68.00. (Right) Cream basketweave biscuit barrel with flower finial, 6¼" tall, Black Mark #1, $48.00 – 68.00.

Plate 112. (Left) Textured biscuit barrel in cream crackle glaze with multicolored fruit motif, 7" tall, Black Mark #1, $48.00 – 68.00. (Right) Basketweave biscuit barrel in yellow shiny glaze with multicolored fruit motif (the grapes have faces on them!), 5½" tall, Black Mark #62A, $48.00 – 68.00.

Plate 113. (Left) Biscuit barrel in yellow shiny glaze with multicolored fruit motif, 6¾" tall, Black Mark #1, $48.00 – 68.00. (Right) Biscuit barrel in red shiny glaze with multicolored fruit motif, 5¾" tall, Black Mark #24, $48.00 – 68.00.

Plate 114. (Left) Biscuit barrel in green shiny glaze with multicolored fruit motif, 6" tall, Black Mark #1, $48.00 – 68.00. (Right) Brown wood-textured biscuit barrel with red berries, 6½" tall, Black Mark #2, $48.00 – 68.00.

Plate 115. (Left) Biscuit barrel in cream and pink shiny glaze with multicolored floral motif, 6¾" tall, Black Mark #1, $48.00 – 68.00. (Right) Biscuit barrel in teal shiny glaze with multicolored floral motif, 8¼" tall, no Mark, $48.00 – 68.00.

Plate 116. (Left) Biscuit barrel in cream shiny glaze with multicolored floral motif, 5¾" tall, Black Mark #1, $48.00 – $68.00. (Right) Biscuit barrel in cream shiny glaze with textured dots and multicolored floral decals, 6" tall, Black Mark #1, $48.00 – 68.00.

Plate 117. Biscuit barrel in cream shiny glaze with multicolored cherries and berries, 7½" tall, Black Mark #1, $48.00 – 68.00.

Plate 118. (Left) Biscuit barrel in cream shiny glaze with multicolored floral motif and pink flower finial, 7½" tall, Black Mark #1, $48.00 – 68.00. (Right) Biscuit barrel in cream and green shiny glaze, 5" tall, Black Mark #29, $48.00 – 68.00.

Plate 119. (Left) Biscuit barrel with basketweave texture in green shiny glaze with multicolored floral motif, 8" tall, $48.00 – 68.00. (Right) Biscuit barrel in green shiny glaze with stippled texture and multicolored floral motif, 4¾" tall, $48.00 – 68.00.

Plate 120. (Left) Biscuit barrel in cream shiny glaze with pink roses, 5½" tall, Black Mark #1, $48.00 – 68.00. (Right) Biscuit barrel in brown and cream shiny glaze with multicolored motif, 6" tall, Black Mark #1, $48.00 – 68.00.

Plate 121. (Left) Biscuit barrel in cream shiny glaze with multicolored floral band, 5½" tall, Black Mark #1, $48.00 – $68.00. (Right) Biscuit barrel in cream shiny glaze with multicolored floral motif, 5¾" tall, Black Mark #3, $48.00 – 68.00.

Plate 122. (Left) Biscuit barrel in cream shiny glaze with multicolored floral motif, 6"
tall, Red Mark #25, $48.00 – 68.00. (Right) Biscuit barrel in cream shiny glaze with
multicolored floral motif, 6" tall, Black Mark #1, $48.00 – 68.00.

Plate 123. Apple biscuit barrel in red semi-matte glaze,
6½" tall, Mark obscured, $48.00 – 68.00.

Plate 124. (Left) Biscuit barrel with people in blue and multicolored shiny glazes, 6½" tall, Black Mark #1, $48.00 – 68.00. (Right) Biscuit barrel with people in blue and multicolored shiny glazes, 7¾" tall, Black Mark #1, $48.00 – 68.00.

Plate 125. (Left) Biscuit barrel with people in cream and multicolored shiny glazes, 6¾" tall, Black Mark #114, $48.00 – 68.00. (Right) Biscuit barrel with people in cream and multicolored shiny glazes, 5" tall, Black Mark #1, $48.00 – 68.00.

⚒ BONZO ⚒

Bonzo was a comic strip and cartoon character from the 1920s through the 1950s. His most popular years were the 1930s.

Plate 126. Bonzo condiment set in yellow luster, tray 7" wide, mustard and tray Red Mark #28, salt and pepper Red Mark #1, $150.00 – 200.00.

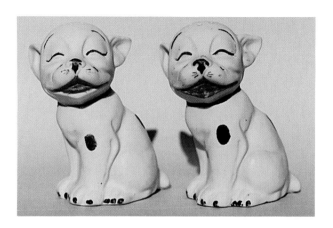

Plate 127. Bonzo bisque salt and pepper, 4½" tall, Black Mark #2, $35.00 – 75.00.

⚒ BOOKENDS ⚒

Plate 128. Colonial bookends in multicolored shiny glaze with blue rhinestone eyes, 6¼" tall, Label #135, $25.00 – 40.00.

Plate 129. Asian man and woman bookends in multicolored shiny glazes, 5½" tall, Green Mark #1, $28.00 – 48.00.

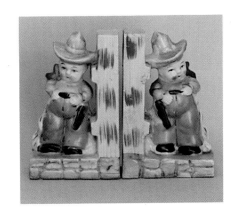

Plate 130. Cowboy bookends in multicolored shiny glazes, 4½" tall, Black Mark #2, $25.00 – 40.00.

Plate 131. Train bookends in black shiny glaze on tan body, 5½" tall, Mark obscured, $20.00 – 30.00.

Plate 132. Ship bookends in multicolored shiny glazes, 6¾" tall, Black Mark #1, $25.00 – 45.00.

Plate 133. Noritake bowl in tan luster glaze with multicolored fruit motif, 8" wide, Green Mark #26, $45.00 – 65.00.

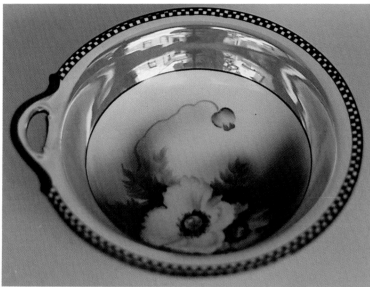

Plate 134. Noritake handled bowl with checkerboard rim and multicolored floral motif, 8" wide, Green Mark #53, $45.00 – 65.00.

Plate 135. Large salad or serving bowl in multicolored luster glazes, 9½" wide, Green Mark #52, $35.00 – 55.00.

Plate 136. Noritake low bowl with scenic motif in multicolored luster and shiny glazes, 9½" wide, Red Mark #36, $45.00 – 65.00.

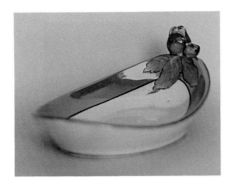

Plate 137. Noritake oval bowl with sprigged-on flower handle in multi-colored luster and shiny glazes, 6¾" long, Red Mark #53, $25.00 – 45.00.

Plate 138. Goldcastle oval bowl in ivory luster with multicolored floral motif, 7¼" long, Red Mark #43, $18.00 – 28.00.

Plate 139. Oval bowl in blue and white luster glaze with multicolored floral motif, 7¾" long, Black Mark #1, $18.00 – 28.00.

Plate 140. (Left) Scenic bowl in multicolored luster glazes *(featured in a 1920s Butler Bros. catalog for $2.00 per dozen)*, 7¼" wide, Black Mark #1, $18.00 – 28.00. (Right) Handled basket in amber luster with multicolored shiny glazes, 7" long, Red Mark #56, $25.00 – 35.00.

Plate 163. Cigarette set in multicolored luster glazes, tray 7½" wide, all Red Mark #25, $175.00 – 225.00.

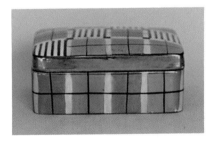

Plate 164. Cigarette box with skirtholder lady in multicolored luster glazes, 4¼" long, Red Mark #25, $75.00 – 125.00.

Plate 165. Cigarette box with lady's face in multicolored shiny glazes, 4¾" long, Black Mark #1, $35.00 – 55.00.

Plate 166. Noritake cigarette box with plaid motif in multicolored luster glazes, 3½" long, Red Mark #53, $75.00 – 100.00.

Plate 143. Scenic bowl with reed handle in multicolored shiny glazes, 7¼" wide, Black Mark #2, $10.00 – 18.00.

Plate 144. Bowl with hand painted Nippon-like motif in orange and multicolored semi-matte glazes, 9½" wide, Red Label with MADE IN JAPAN, $20.00 – 35.00.

Plate 145. Footed bowl with Hand Painted Nippon-like motif in multi-colored semi-matte glazes (probably from the transitional period between the Nippon and Made in Japan Eras, especially in light of the decoration around the border), 6½" wide, Red Mark #1, $20.00 – 35.00.

Plate 146. Bowl with dog in multicolored shiny glazes, 3¼" tall, Black Mark #2, $20.00 – 35.00.

Plate 147. Goldcastle calico dog ashtray, 4½" wide, Red Mark #43, $25.00 – 40.00.

Plate 148. Calico baby and mother bird ashtray, 2¾" tall, Red Mark #1, $25.00 – 40.00.

Plate 149. Calico dog with card suit heart ashtray, 2¾" tall, Black Mark #1, $18.00 – 28.00.

Plate 150. Calico dog ashtray, 2¾" tall, Black Mark #1, $18.00 – 28.00.

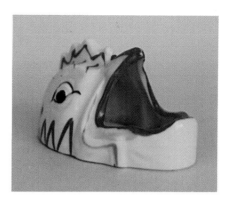

Plate 152. Calico chicken face ashtray, 3¾" long, Black Mark #1 and #38, Blind Mark #1 and #38, $25.00 – 35.00.

Plate 151. Calico cat ashtray, 3½", Black Mark #2, $25.00 – 35.00.

Plate 153. Calico dog pincushion, 2" tall, Black Mark #38, $28.00 – $38.00.

Plate 154. (Left) Calico chicken cache pot, 4¼" tall, Red Mark #1, $20.00 – 30.00. (Right) Calico elephant pincushion, 2¾" tall, Black Mark #1, $28.00 – 38.00.

Plate 155. Candlesticks in multicolored luster glazes with butterfly motif, 4" wide, Red Mark #25, pair $30.00 – 65.00.

Plate 156. Candlesticks with flowers in multicolored luster glazes, 4" wide, Red Mark #25, pair $30.00 – 65.00.

Plate 157. Noritake chambersticks with scenic motif in multicolored shiny glazes, 1¾" tall, Red Mark #53, pair $80.00 – 100.00

Plate 158. Noritake chambersticks with floral motif in multicolored shiny glazes, 1¾" tall, Red Mark #53, pair $80.00 – $100.00.

Plate 159. Candlesticks in white shiny glaze, 3¼" tall, Black Mark #1, pair $8.00 – 12.00.

Plate 160. Candlesticks in orange shiny glaze with blue and white floral motif, 5½" tall, Black Mark #52, pair $30.00 – 50.00.

Plate 161. Candlestick in multicolored shiny glazes, 6¼" tall, Gold Mark #1, $18.00 – 28.00.

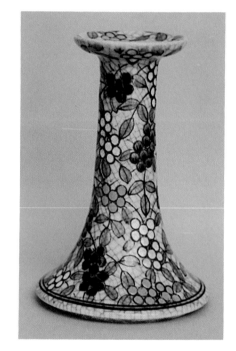

Plate 162. Altar boy candleholder in multicolored shiny glazes, 6" tall, Blue and White Label with JAPAN, and stamped "San Myro" in red, $20.00 – 35.00.

Plate 163. Cigarette set in multicolored luster glazes, tray 7½" wide, all Red Mark #25, $175.00 – 225.00.

Plate 164. Cigarette box with skirtholder lady in multicolored luster glazes, 4¼" long, Red Mark #25, $75.00 – 125.00.

Plate 165. Cigarette box with lady's face in multicolored shiny glazes, 4¾" long, Black Mark #1, $35.00 – 55.00.

Plate 166. Noritake cigarette box with plaid motif in multicolored luster glazes, 3½" long, Red Mark #53, $75.00 – 100.00.

Plate 167. Cigarette box with elephant finial in multicolored shiny glazes, 4½" long, Red Mark #1, $30.00 – 45.00.

Plate 168. Cigarette box with Tree in the Meadow motif in multicolored shiny glazes, 4" long, Black Mark #1, $25.00 – 40.00.

Plate 169. Cigarette boxes with dog finials in multicolored semi-matte glazes, 3¼" long, both Black Mark #2, $20.00 – 30.00 each.

The debate continues whether to call these items cigarette or card holders. I believe they were sold as both. However, in the 1934 movie "Jimmy the Gent," Bette Davis asks her co-star to get her "a deck of cigarettes!"

Plate 170. Noritake cigarette or card holder with playing card motif in multicolored luster glazes, 3¾" tall, Red Mark #53, $100.00 – 150.00.

Plate 171. Cigarette or card holder with playing card motif in multicolored shiny glazes, 3¼" tall, Red Mark #1, $25.00 – $45.00.

Plate 172. Cigarette or card holder in multicolored luster glazes, 4¾" tall, Black Mark #56, $40.00 – $65.00.

Plate 173. Noritake cigarette holder in multicolored luster glazes, 4¾" tall, Green Mark #53, $90.00 – $125.00.

Plate 174. Cigarette holder with onion dome in multicolored shiny glazes, 7" tall, Black Mark #115, $65.00 – 85.00.

Plate 175. Clown cigarette holder with three stacking ashtrays in multicolored shiny glazes, clown Red Mark #1, yellow ashtray Red Mark #1 and Black Mark #1, red ashtray Black Mark #1, green ashtray no Mark, set as pictured $40.00 – 60.00 ($50.00 – 75.00 if complete with four or six ashtrays).

Plate 176. Cigarette holder with one stacking ashtray in multicolored shiny glazes, both Black Mark #1, as pictured $18.00 – 28.00 ($30.00 – 45.00 if complete with four ashtrays).

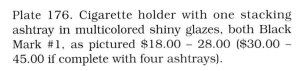

Plate 177. Bear cigarette holders in multicolored shiny glazes with floral decals, 4½" tall, left Red Mark #1, right Red Mark #25, $10.00 – 15.00 as pictured ($45.00 – 65.00 if complete with four stacking ashtrays).

Plate 178. Tobacco humidor with opening in head for dampened sponge (to keep the tobacco moist) in multicolored luster glazes, 6" tall, Red Mark #12A, $85.00 – 155.00.

Plate 178a. Detail of opening for dampened sponge.

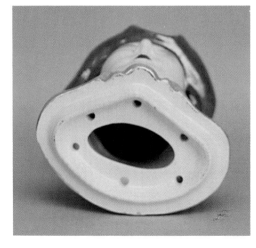

Plate 179. Bird condiment set in multicolored luster glazes, tray 7¾" wide, all Black Mark #1, $125.00 – 150.00.

Plate 180. Condiment set in blue luster glaze with white shiny glaze floral motif, tray 7" in diameter, toothpick holder Mark #52, other pieces no Mark, $65.00 – 125.00.

Plate 181. Condiment set in multicolored shiny glazes, tray 7¾" wide, Black Mark #21, $65.00 – 125.00.

Plate 182. Condiment set in multicolored luster glazes, tray 9¼" wide, tray and mustard Black Mark #52, oil and vinegar Red Mark #52, salt and pepper no Mark, $65.00 – 125.00.

Plate 183. Condiment set in multicolored shiny glazes, tray 5½" wide, tray and toothpick holder Red Mark #52, salt and pepper and mustard no Mark, $65.00 – 105.00.

Plate 184. Airplane condiment set in white opal luster, 7½" long, Label with Sarsaparilla Deco Designs N.Y.C.N.Y. © 1981 JAPAN, $20.00 – 30.00.

Plate 185. Angular condiment set in blue, tan, and multicolored luster glazes, tray 6¼" wide, tray and mustard Black Mark #21, salt and pepper Black Mark #1, $35.00 – 45.00.

Plate 186. "Motto ware" condiment set in multicolored shiny glazes *(shown in the 1932 Sears catalog for 79¢ per set)*, tray 5¼" wide with Black Mark #30, salt, pepper and mustard all Black Mark #1, 40.00 – $80.00.

Plate 187. Scenic condiment set on deep tray in multicolored luster glazes *(shown in the 1929 Sears catalog with a different motif for $1.00 per set)*, tray 5¼" long, mustard and tray Red Mark #32, salt and pepper Red Mark #1, $30.00 – 65.00.

Plate 188. Condiment set with butterfly finial in multicolored luster glazes, 2¾" tall, all Black Mark #1, $30.00 – 50.00.

Plate 189. Condiment set in tan and blue luster glazes, tray 4½" wide with Black Mark #1; salt, pepper, and mustard no Mark, $30.00 – 40.00.

Plate 190. Noritake condiment set in red and black shiny glazes, tray 3¾" wide, mustard and tray Green Mark #53; salt and pepper no Mark, $65.00 – 85.00.

Plate 191. Condiment set with bird and grain motif in yellow matte and blue luster glazes *(shown in the 1927 Sears catalog with a different motif for $1.00)*, tray 4½" wide, mustard and tray Red Mark #1; salt and pepper no Mark, $30.00 – 45.00.

Plate 192. Girl with flowers condiment set in multicolored shiny glazes *(pictured in a 1920s Butler Brothers catalog as part of an assortment of one dozen sets for $5.40 per dozen)*, 3¾" tall, all Blind Mark #1, $125.00 – 150.00.

Plate 193. Rabbit condiment set in blue luster and orange shiny glaze, tray 7" wide with Green Mark #25, mustard Green Mark #1, salt Black Mark #1, and pepper Black Mark #2, $45.00 – 85.00.

Plate 194. Penguin condiment set in multicolored shiny glazes, 7" tall, all Black Mark #1, $35.00 – 55.00.

Plate 195. Donkey condiment set in multicolored shiny glazes, 7¼" tall, Label #136, $15.00 – 25.00.

Plate 196. Mustard and horseradish condiment set in multicolored shiny glazes, 4¼" tall, Black Mark #2, $25.00 – 45.00.

Plate 197. Cream and sugar on tray in multicolored luster glazes *(pictured in a 1920s Butler Brothers catalog with a different motif for 65¢),* tray 6½" wide, all Green Mark #1, $35.00 – 50.00.

Plate 198. Cream and sugar on tray in tan and multicolored luster glazes, tray 7¼" wide, all Red Mark #25, $35.00 – 50.00.

Plate 199. Cream and sugar on tray in multicolored luster glazes, tray 7¼" wide, Mark obscured, $35.00 – 50.00.

Plate 200. Cream and sugar on tray in green oilspot glaze, tray 7½" wide with Green Mark #116; cream and sugar Black Mark #25, $35.00 – 50.00.

Plate 201. Cowboy cream and sugar in multicolored shiny glazes, sugar 3" tall, both Red Mark #1, $40.00 – 65.00.

Plate 202. Dog cream and sugar with yellow eyes, in multicolored luster glazes 6¾" tall, Black Mark #1, $100.00 – 150.00.

Plate 203. Duck cream and sugar in multicolored luster and shiny glazes, 3¼" tall, Red Mark #25, $45.00 – 75.00.

Plate 204. Foo dog cream and sugar in black and white shiny glaze, 4" tall, Black Mark #1, $35.00 – 50.00.

Plate 205. Maruyama clown egg timer in multi-colored shiny glazes, 3½" tall, Red Mark #65, $30.00 – 45.00.

Plate 206. (Left) Girl egg timer in multicolored shiny glazes, 3¼" tall, Black Mark #40, $30.00 – 45.00. (Right) Boy egg timer in multicolored shiny glazes, 3¼" tall, Black Mark #40, $30.00 – 45.00.

Plate 207. Chef egg timer in multicolored luster and shiny glazes, 3¼" tall, Red Mark #40, $30.00 – 45.00.

Plate 208. Large egg timer in multicolored shiny glazes, 5" tall, Black Mark #1, $30.00 – 45.00.

Plate 209. Maruyama Dutch girl egg timer in multicolored shiny glazes, 3¾" tall, Red Mark #65, $30.00 – 45.00.

Plate 210. Colonial lady figurine in multicolored shiny glazes (a most versatile blank: it's a powder box in Plate 466 and a vase in Plate 597 of Book 2 of *The Collector's Guide to Made in Japan Ceramics*, and it was also made into an incense burner!), 7" tall, Red Mark #1, $30.00 – 45.00.

Plate 211. Dancing lady figurine in pink and green shiny glaze, 4½" tall, Black Mark #1, $40.00 – 60.00.

Plate 212. Set of four bisque doll figurines in original box, 3¾" tall, all have Red Mark #2 on one foot, boy Blind Mark #1; pink girl incised SS 74 and Blind Mark #1; green girl incised SS 74 and Black Mark #2; orange girl incised SS75 and Blind Mark #1; set $100.00 – 150.00.

Plate 213. Bisque doll figurine in wig and blue dress, 6½" tall, Blind Mark #2, $35.00 – 55.00.

Plate 214. Set of two skier figurines in multicolored semi-matte glazes, 5½" tall, Red Mark #1, pair $30.00 – 50.00.

Plate 215. Bellhop figurine in multicolored shiny glazes, 5" tall, Red Mark #18, $20.00 – 30.00.

Plate 216. Cowboy figurine in multicolored shiny glazes, 4" tall, Blind Mark #2, $20.00 – 30.00.

Plate 217. Barefoot boy figurine in multicolored shiny glazes, 4¾" tall, Blue Mark #57, $35.00 – 50.00.

Plate 218. Boy and bird figurine in multicolored shiny glazes, 3" tall, Mark #2, $12.00 – 22.00.

Plate 219. Boy and dogs figurine in multicolored shiny glazes, 4" tall, Mark #2, $12.00 – 22.00.

Plate 220. (Left) Soldier figurine in multicolored shiny glazes 5" tall, Red Mark #2, $18.00 – 28.00. (Right) Clown figurine in opal luster and multicolored shiny glazes, 5¼" tall, Black Mark #18, $18.00 – 28.00.

Plate 221. Set of three musician figurines in multicolored shiny glazes, 2¾" tall, all Red Mark #1, $10.00 – $18.00 each.

Plate 222. Bisque pixie figurine with accordion in multicolored matte glazes, 4¾" tall, Red Mark #1, $20.00 – 30.00.

Plate 223. Pixie on butterfly figurine in multicolored shiny glazes, 3½" tall, Green Mark #1, $25.00 – 40.00.

Plate 224. (Left) Flower lady figurine with accordion in multicolored shiny glazes, 4½" tall, Red Mark #23, $18.00 – 28.00. (Right) Dog figurine in multicolored shiny glazes, 4¼" tall, Black Mark #2, $18.00 – 28.00.

Plate 255. Mini flower bowl with frog in orange shiny glaze with white moriage fish motif, 3¾" wide, Black Mark #1, $15.00 – 20.00.

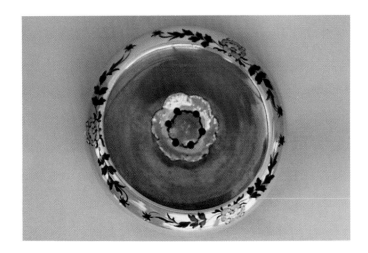

Plate 256. Flower bowl with frog in multicolored luster glazes, 6" wide, Mark obscured, $18.00 – 28.00.

Plate 257. Swan flower bowl with frog in multicolored luster glaze, 4" tall, Black Mark #1, $50.00 – 80.00.

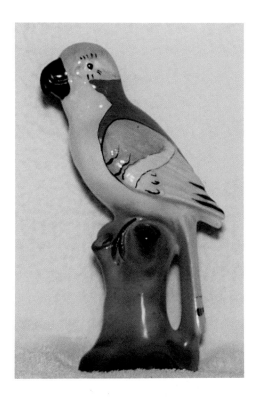

Plate 258. Flower bowl with crab flower frog in purple shiny glaze, 7½" wide, Blind Mark #2, $50.00 – 80.00.

Plate 259. Bird flower frog in multicolored luster and shiny glazes, 7½" tall, Mark #2, $30.00 – 45.00.

Plate 261. Egyptian lady incense burner in gold luster glaze, 9¾" long, Red Mark #2, $40.00 – 50.00 as pictured ($55.00 – 75.00 with domed cage that fits over the bowl).

Plate 260. Japanese lady with dog incense burner in multicolored luster glazes, 4¾" tall, Black Mark #52, $40.00 – 50.00 as pictured ($55.00 – 75.00 with domed cage that fits over the bowl).

Plate 263. Asian man incense burner in multicolored shiny glazes, 5" tall, Black Mark #1 and Blind Mark #38, $20.00 – 30.00.

Plate 262. Buddha incense burner in multicolored luster glazes with matchholder and slot for storing joss or incense, 5¼" long, Black Mark #25, $50.00 – 75.00.

Plate 264. "'Pon My Soul" bisque incense burner in multicolored shiny glazes with label from Merriman's, a shop in Seaside, Oregon, that closed about 1952, 4½" wide, Black Mark #1, $30.00 – 50.00.

Plate 265. Large dog on book incense burner in multicolored shiny glazes, 7" tall, Black Mark #73A, $75.00 – 100.00.

Plate 266. House incense burner in multicolored shiny glazes, 5" tall, Blind Mark #1, $18.00 – 28.00.

Plate 267. Fieldstone fireplace incense burner in multicolored matte glazes, 4½" tall, no Mark. (I have seen two of these, both with no Mark, so they may have had labels, or perhaps they were not Made in Japan.) $15.00 – 25.00.

Plate 268. Fireplace incense burner in black and red shiny glaze, 4" tall, Red Mark #1, $15.00 – 25.00.

269a. Detail of liner and domed cage.

Plate 269. Bird-handled incense burner with liner and domed cage in multicolored luster glazes, 5¾" tall, Red Mark #25, $35.00 – 55.00.

Plate 270. Kinkozan incense burner in multicolored shiny glazes, 5½" tall, Red Mark #49, $45.00 – 65.00.

Plate 271. Incense burner in multicolored shiny glazes, 4¼" tall, Red Mark #117, $45.00 – 65.00.

Plate 272. Noritake lemon server with tulip motif in multicolored semi-matte glazes, 6¼" wide, Red Mark #53, $35.00-55.00.

Plate 273. Noritake lemon server with zigzag and floral motif in tan luster and multicolored shiny glazes, 5¾" wide, Red Mark #53, $35.00 – 55.00.

Plate 274. Noritake lemon server with house motif in multicolored shiny glazes, 5½" wide, Red Mark #53, $35.00 – 55.00.

Plate 275. Noritake scenic lemon server in multicolored shiny glazes with blue luster rim, 5¾" wide, Red Mark #53, $25.00 – 40.00.

Plate 276. Noritake lemon server in multicolored shiny glazes, 5½" wide, Red Mark #53, $20.00 – 30.00.

Plate 277. Noritake flower-shaped lemon server in multicolored shiny glazes, 5¾" wide, Green Mark #53, $20.00 – 30.00.

Plate 278. Noritake Tree in the Meadow lemon server in multicolored semi-matte glazes, 5½" wide, Blue Mark #53A, $20.00 – 30.00.

Plate 279. Noritake octagonal lemon server in green and multicolored semi-matte glazes, 5¾" wide, Red Mark #53, $20.00 – 30.00.

Plate 280. Lemon server with bird handle in orange and white shiny glaze, 6" wide, Red Mark #50, $25.00 – 35.00.

Plate 281. Lemon server with floral handle in multicolored shiny glazes, 6" wide, Red Mark #25, $25.00 – 35.00.

Plate 282. Lemon server with Mexican motif in multicolored shiny glazes, 5½" wide, Red Mark #47, $25.00 – 35.00.

Plate 283. Lemon server in multicolored semi-matte glazes, 6¼" wide, Black Mark #63, $20.00 – 30.00.

Plate 284. Japanese bisque liquor flask inscribed "Give me a wee o'light" in multi-colored matte and shiny glazes, 4" tall, Black Mark #1 and Blind Mark #1, $75.00 – 135.00.

Plate 285. German bisque liquor flask inscribed "A WEE SCOTCH" in multi-colored matte and shiny glazes, 4¼" tall, no Mark, $85.00 – 150.00.

Note that the Japanese flask is very similar in quality, design, and glazing to the German one. In fact, if it were not backstamped with the Made in Japan Mark, the Japanese flask could easily be mistaken for a German one.

Plate 286. Elephant decanter with four shot glasses in brown and multicolored shiny glazes on brown body, 8" wide, Label #112A, set $20.00 – 30.00.

Plate 287. Lefton china mustache man decanter with two shot glasses (shown front and back) in multicolored semi-matte glazes, 7¼" tall, Label 58A, set $20.00 – 30.00.

Plate 288. Two corks in multicolored shiny glazes, 2" tall, Black Mark #2, set $35.00 – 50.00.

Majolica is pottery made of earthenware with colorful, metal-based glazes usually containing tin. "True" Majolica was made in the Victorian era, from about 1850 until 1900, mainly in England and America. Other countries produced it as well, and versions of Majolica have been made fairly continually right up until the present time, including pieces of reproduction Victorian Majolica that currently seem to be at every flea market and antique show on the West Coast. (These are not repros of Japanese Majolica, and they are not made in Japan.)

There are three schools of thought about Japanese Majolica. The first school feels that it is not "true" Majolica because it was made later and the quality is not always as fine as the Victorian era Majolica. The second school feels that since virtually every ceramics-producing country made it over such a long span of time, the Japanese ware is just as "true" as any other Majolica. The third school just doesn't care!

It is interesting to note that Victorian era Majolica producers borrowed heavily from Japanese pottery that was so popular at the time. With its natural and figural motifs, it is easy to see the Japanese influence in Victorian Majolica. So it is ironic that the Japanese pieces which echo or copy the Victorian era Majolica pieces are really copies of ideas and designs that were borrowed from Japan in the first place. What a conundrum! So, to save everybody's sanity, let's just call the Japanese ware "Majolica-style!"

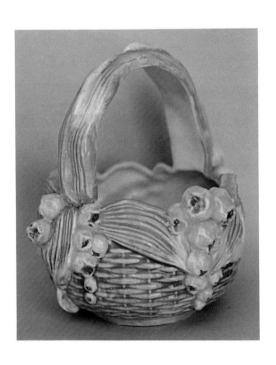

Plate 289. Majolica-style basket with floral motif in multicolored shiny glazes, 7" tall, Black Mark #35, $65.00 – 85.00.

Plate 290. Majolica-style basket with fruit in multicolored shiny glazes, 6¾" tall, Black Mark #1, $65.00 – 85.00.

Plate 291. Majolica-style basket in red and green shiny glaze, 6" wide, Black Mark #73A, $25.00 – 35.00.

Plate 292. Majolica-style bowl with insect handle in multicolored shiny glazes, 6" wide, Blind Mark #1, $45.00 – 65.00.

Plate 293. Majolica-style bowl with sprigged-on cherries in green and red shiny glaze, 6¼" long, Blind Mark #1, $25.00 – $35.00.

Plate 294. Majolica-style Dutch girl cache pot or vace in multicolored shiny glazes (flower pot is glazed onto the pedestal base), 5½" tall, Black Mark #1, $25.00 – 40.00.

Plate 295. Majolica-style camel cache pot or vase in multicolored shiny glazes, 8" wide, Black Mark #1, $45.00 – 65.00.

Plate 296. Majolica-style bird cache pot in multicolored shiny glazes, 3¾" wide, Blind Mark #1, $35.00 – 45.00.

Plate 297. Majolica-style bird and worm cache pot in multicolored shiny glazes, 6" tall, Black Mark #2, $35.00 – 45.00.

Plate 298. Majolica-style owl cream and sugar in multicolored shiny glazes, sugar is 4¾" tall, Black Mark #1, $35.00 – 55.00.

Plate 299. Majolica-style seated man figure in multicolored shiny glazes, 7½" tall, Blind Mark #1, $85.00 – 95.00.

Plate 300. Majolica-style flower bowl in multicolored shiny glazes, 8½" wide, no Mark, $25.00 – 35.00.

Plate 301. Majolica-style owl flower frog in multicolored shiny glazes, 6" tall, Black Mark #1, $40.00 – 50.00.

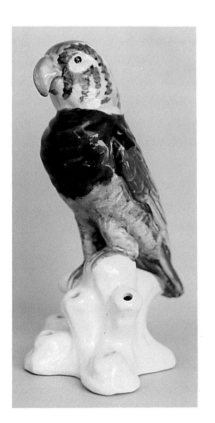

Plate 302. Majolica-style bird flower frog in multicolored shiny glazes, 8¾" tall, Blind Mark #1, $60.00 – 75.00.

Plate 303. Majolica-style bird flower frog in green and multicolored shiny glazes, 5¾" tall, Blind Mark #1, $40.00 – 50.00.

Plate 304. Majolica-style bird flower frog in multicolored shiny glazes, 4½" tall, Mark obscured, $30.00 – 45.00.

Plate 305. Majolica-style bird flower frog in multicolored matte glazes, 6" tall, Blind Mark #1, $30.00 – 45.00.

Plate 306. Majolica-style bird flower frog in multicolored matte glazes, 4" tall, Blind Mark #85, $30.00 – 45.00.

Plate 307. Majolica-style flower frog with house and tree in multicolored semi-matte glazes, 4" tall, no Mark, $30.00 – 45.00.

Plate 308. Majolica-style bird flower frog-like vase (the bottom is enclosed, so it is not truly a flower frog, yet the holes are so large and regular that it could even be a pencil holder—another one of the mysteries of Made in Japan collecting!) in multicolored shiny glazes, 7¾" tall, Blind Mark #1, $30.00 – 45.00.

Plate 309. Majolica-style lemon server with blown-out leaves and flower and applied lemon in multicolored shiny glazes, 6" wide, Black Mark #1, $30.00 – 45.00.

Plate 310. Majolica-style salt and pepper on leaf tray in multicolored shiny glazes, salt and pepper no Mark; tray Black Mark #40, $25.00 – 35.00.

Plate 311. Majolica-style large fruit salt and pepper in basket in multicolored shiny glazes (*a similar set was advertised in the 1930 Sears catalog as "Banko China"*), 4" tall, Blind Mark #1, $30.00 – 50.00.

Plate 312. Majolica-style flower salt and pepper in multicolored shiny glazes, 5¼" wide, all Black Mark #2, $20.00 – $35.00.

Plate 313. Majolica-style bird nester salt and pepper in multicolored shiny glazes, 3½" wide, tree Red Mark #2; salt and pepper Black Mark #2, $20.00 – 35.00.

Plate 314. Majolica-style turkey nester salt and pepper in multicolored shiny glazes, 4½" wide, nest no Mark; salt and pepper Black Mark #2, $20.00 – 35.00.

Plate 315. Majolica-style frog and strawberries salt and pepper in multicolored shiny glazes, 4" tall, frog and one shaker Black Mark #2; one shaker Red Mark #2, $45.00 – 65.00.

Plate 316. Majolica-style teapot with cream and sugar in multicolored shiny glazes, (the woodsy motif puts this set in the Majolica-style category, but the un-Majolica cuteness of the flowers almost puts it back out again) pot 4½" tall, all Black Mark #1, set $25.00 – 35.00.

Plate 317. Majolica-style biscuit barrel in multi-colored shiny glazes, 5½" tall, Black Mark #1, $48.00 – 68.00.

Plate 318. Majolica-style three-bird vase in multicolored shiny glazes, 7¼" tall, Black Mark #1, $85.00 – 125.00.

Plate 319. Majolica-style bird vase in multicolored shiny glazes, 5¾" tall, Blind Mark #1 (with a blue circle-shaped Mark that is too smeary to read), $35.00 – 50.00.

Plate 320. Majolica-style bird vase in blue and multicolored shiny glazes, 8½" tall, Blind Mark #1, $50.00 – 65.00.

Plate 321. Majolica-style double tree bud vase in multicolored shiny glazes, 7½" wide, Blind Mark #1, $50.00 – 65.00.

Plate 322. Majolica-style bird vase in multicolored shiny glazes, 5½" tall, Black Mark #1, $30.00 – 45.00.

Plate 323. Majolica-style floral hanging vase in multicolored shiny glazes, 6½" deep, Black Mark #80, $85.00 – 100.00.

Plate 324. Majolica-style parrot hanging vase in multicolored shiny glazes, 9¾" tall, Black Mark #2, $85.00 – 100.00.

Plate 325. Majolica-style double parrot hanging vase in multicolored shiny glazes, 9" tall, Black Mark #1, $35.00 – 60.00.

Plate 326. Majolica-style circular hanging vase with bird motif in multicolored shiny glazes, 7½" in diameter, Blind Mark #1, $35.00 – 45.00.

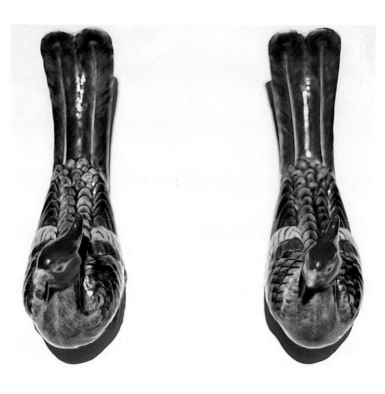

Plate 327. Majolica-style circular hanging vase with bird and floral motif in multicolored shiny glazes, 7" tall, Blind Mark #1, $50.00 – 75.00.

Plate 328. Very large pair of Majolica-style bird wall pockets in multicolored shiny glazes, 10½" long, Red Mark #1, pair $130.00 – 170.00.

Plate 329. Majolica-style peacock wall pocket in multicolored shiny glazes, 5¼" long, Blind Mark #1, $65.00 – 85.00.

Plate 330. Majolica-style duck and flower wall pocket in multicolored shiny glazes, 5¼" long, Black Mark #1, $65.00 – 85.00.

Plate 331. Majolica-style owl wall pocket in multicolored shiny glazes, 7¼" long, Black Mark #1, $65.00 – 85.00.

Plate 332. Majolica-style bird and flowers wall pocket in multicolored shiny glazes, 6" long, Blind Mark #1, $65.00 – 85.00.

Plate 333. Majolica-style bird wall pocket in multicolored shiny glazes, 6" long, no Mark, $35.00 – 55.00.

Plate 334. Majolica-style bird and grapes wall pocket in multicolored shiny glazes, 7¼" long, Blind Mark #1, $35.00 – 55.00.

Plate 335. Majolica-style wall pocket with bird in blue and multicolored shiny glazes, 7" long, Blind Mark #1, $35.00 – 55.00.

Plate 336. Majolica-style wall pocket with bird and flowers in cream and multicolored shiny glazes, 7½" long, Black Mark #1, $35.00 – 55.00.

Plate 337. Majolica-style bird and berries wall pocket in multicolored semi-matte glazes, 7" long, Blind Mark #1, $30.00 – 50.00.

Plate 338. Majolica-style bird wall pocket in multicolored shiny glazes, 6¾" long, Mark obscured, $30.00 – 50.00.

Plate 339. Majolica-style wall pocket with bird motif in multicolored shiny glazes, 8" tall, Black Mark #1, $35.00 – 55.00.

Plate 340. Majolica-style wall pocket with pineapple motif in multicolored shiny glazes, 7¾" tall, Blind Mark #1, $35.00 – 55.00.

Plate 341. Majolica-style wall pocket in green shiny glazes with maroon flower, 5½" long, Blind Mark #1, $30.00 – 45.00.

Plate 342. Majolica-style wall pocket in green shiny glaze with yellow flower, 6" long, Black Mark #1, $30.00 – 45.00.

Plate 343. Majolica-style wall pocket in blue shiny glaze with multicolored floral motif, 5½" long, Blind Mark #1, $40.00 – 60.00.

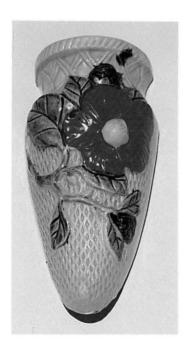

Plate 344. Majolica-style wall pocket in yellow shiny glaze with red floral motif, 7" long, Green Mark #1, $35.00 – 55.00.

Plate 345. Majolica-style wall pocket with flower and butterfly in yellow and multicolored shiny glazes, 7¼" long, no Mark, $30.00 – 45.00.

Plate 346. Majolica-style wall pocket (with front cut away to form basket shape) in multicolored shiny glazes, 6½" long, Blind Mark #1, $35.00 – 50.00.

Plate 347. (Left) Majolica-style basket wall pocket in multicolored shiny glazes, 8½" long, Blind Mark #1, $45.00 – 65.00. (Right) Majolica-style basket wall pocket in multicolored shiny glazes, 9" long, Black Mark #1, $45.00 – 65.00.

Plate 348. Majolica-style wall pocket with grapes in multicolored shiny glazes, 6¼" long, Black Mark #1, $20.00 – 30.00.

Plate 349. Marmalade or jam pot and liner plate in tan luster glaze with black silhouettes of trees and dancers, plate 6½" wide, plate and pot Red Mark #21A; spoon Red Mark #11, $85.00 – 125.00.

Plate 350. Marmalade or jam pot with dog finial and liner plate in multicolored luster and shiny glazes, 5¼" tall, Red Mark #52, $60.00 – 90.00.

Plate 351. Marmalade or jam pot with bee finial and attached liner plate in multicolored luster and shiny glazes, 6½" wide, Black Mark #1, $25.00 – 45.00.

Plate 352. Noritake marmalade or jam pot with fruit motif in multicolored luster glazes, 4¾" tall, Red Mark #26, $25.00 – 35.00 as pictured ($55.00 – 70.00 with liner plate).

Plate 353. Bisque policeman nodder ashtray in multicolored matte glazes, 4½" tall, Black Mark #1, $95.00 – 125.00.

Plate 354. Hens condiment set nodder in multi-colored shiny glazes, 5" wide, salt and pepper no Mark but "PATENT TT," base Green Mark #23A, $65.00 – 95.00.

Plate 355. Masonic composition figural nodder, 6" tall, Label with MALK EXCLUSIVE MADE IN JAPAN, $100.00 – 135.00.

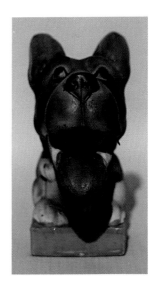

Plate 356. Dog figural nodder in multicolored semi-matte glazes, 4½" tall, Black Mark #1 with Patent Number 54256 (a 1926 patent number), $95.00 – 135.00.

Plate 357. Bird figural nodder in multicolored luster and shiny glazes, 3¼" tall, Red Mark #1, $95.00 – $125.00.

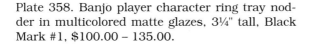

Plate 358. Banjo player character ring tray nodder in multicolored matte glazes, 3¼" tall, Black Mark #1, $100.00 – 135.00.

Plate 359. Black cat salt and pepper nodder in multicolored shiny glazes, 3¾" tall, Red Mark #1, $100.00 – 150.00.

⨔ NUT CUPS ⨔

Plate 360. Nut set in black and blue shiny glaze, master nut 5" wide, all Black Mark #1, $35.00 – 65.00.

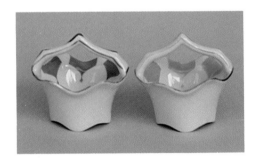

Plate 362. Bunny nut cup in multicolored shiny glazes, 2½" tall, Red Mark #2, $18.00 – 28.00.

Plate 361. Goldcastle nut cups in multicolored shiny glazes, 2½" tall, Red Mark #43, $18.00 – 28.00 each.

Plate 363. Rooster nut cup in multicolored shiny glazes, 2½" tall, Black Mark #2, $18.00 – 28.00

Plate 364. Clown perfume in multicolored shiny glazes *(shown in the 1931 Sears Catalog as part of a pair, the other piece being the Dutch Boy perfume in Plate 567 of The Collector's Guide to Made in Japan Ceramics, Book 2)*, 3½" tall, Red Mark #25, $125.00 – 150.00.

Plate 365. Rabbit perfume in amber and white luster glaze, 3½" tall, Red Mark #25, $125.00 – 150.00.

Plate 366. Perfume set in metal holder with boat motif in multicolored luster and shiny glazes, 6½" tall, bottles Red Mark #25; holder Blind Mark #1, set $65.00 – 95.00.

Plate 367. Perfume set in metal holder with floral motif in multicolored luster and shiny glazes, 6½" tall, bottles Red Mark #25; holder Blind Mark #1, set $65.00 – 95.00.

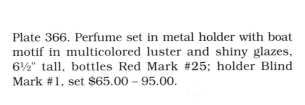

Plate 368. Meito perfume bottle in multicolored shiny glazes, 4" tall, Red and Green Mark #64, $25.00 – 45.00.

Plate 369. Pincushion doll with china feet and legs in multicolored luster and shiny glazes, 5" tall, Red Mark #1, $50.00 – 75.00.

Plate 370. Dutch girl pincushion with thimble in multicolored luster and shiny glazes, 3½" tall, Red Mark #1, $45.00 – 65.00.

Plate 371. (Left) Bisque girl with basket pincushion in multicolored matte glazes, 3" tall, Blind Mark #1, $30.00 – 40.00. (Right) Bathing beauty on shell pincushion in multicolored shiny glazes, 2½" tall, Red Mark #1, $45.00 – 55.00.

Plate 372. (Left) Girl in canoe pincushion in multicolored luster and shiny glazes, 2¼" tall, Red Mark #40, $30.00 – 40.00. (Right) Bisque boy pincushion in multicolored shiny glazes, 3" tall, Blind Mark #1, $30.00 – 40.00.

Plate 373. Skier pincushion in multicolored shiny glazes, 3¼" tall, Red Mark #2, $18.00 – 28.00.

Plate 374. Colonial gentleman with dog pincushion in multicolored shiny glazes, 4" tall, Black Mark #2, $18.00 – 28.00.

Plate 375. Black child pincushion in multicolored luster and shiny glazes, 2¾" tall, Black Mark #2, $50.00 – 75.00.

Plate 376. Bird on flower pincushion in multicolored luster and shiny glazes, 3½" tall, Black Mark #1, $18.00 – 28.00.

Plate 377. Bird pincushion in multicolored luster and shiny glazes, 3¾" tall, Black Mark #1, $25.00 – 35.00.

Plate 378. Bird pincushion or cache pot in multicolored luster glazes, 2½" tall, Black Mark #1, $18.00 – 28.00.

Plate 379. Duck pincushion in multicolored luster and shiny glazes, 2½" tall, Red Mark #1, $18.00 – 28.00.

Plate 380. Swan pincushion in multicolored luster and shiny glazes, 3¼" tall, Red Mark #1, $20.00 – 30.00.

Plate 381. Chicken and bunny pincushion in multicolored shiny glazes, 3¼" tall, Black Mark #1, $18.00 – 28.00.

Plate 382. (Left) Bird with mushrooms pincushion in multicolored matte and shiny glazes, 3¾" tall, Black Mark #1, $18.00 – 28.00. (Center) Tiger with card suit pincushion in yellow matte glaze, 3¼" tall, Red Mark #1, $18.00 – 28.00. (Right) Dog pincushion in pink and blue shiny glaze, 4¾" tall, Black Mark #1, $18.00 – 28.00.

Plate 383. Scottie pincushion in gray and white shiny glaze, 2½" tall, Black Mark #2, $20.00 – 30.00.

Plate 384. Dog family pincushion in multicolored shiny glazes, 2" tall, Red Mark #1 and Blind Mark #45, $18.00 – 28.00.

Plate 385. (Left) Elephant pincushion in tan luster and multicolored matte glazes, 2¼" tall, Black Mark #1, $18.00 – 28.00. (Center) Dog and flower pincushion in multicolored matte glazes, 2¼" tall, Red Mark #1, $18.00 – 28.00. (Right) Donkey pincushion in multicolored shiny glazes used as a table favor with a name cold painted on it, 2" tall, Black Mark #2, $18.00 – 28.00.

Plate 386. Animal card suit pincushion in multicolored luster and shiny glazes, 4½" tall, Black Mark #38, $18.00 – 28.00.

Plate 387. (Left) Giraffe pincushion in multicolored shiny glazes, 2½" tall, Black Mark #1, $25.00 – 35.00. (Right) Dog pincushion in multicolored shiny glazes, 2¼" tall, Black Mark #1, $25.00 – 35.00.

Plate 388. Camel pincushion in yellow and tan luster glaze, 2" tall, Blind Mark #2, $18.00 – 28.00.

Plate 389. Large ram pincushion or cache pot in multicolored luster and shiny glazes, 5½" wide, Black Mark #1, $18.00 – 28.00.

Plate 390. Toby jug pitcher in multicolored shiny glazes, 6¼" tall, Green Mark 60A, $25.00 – 45.00.

Plate 391. Large Mickey Mouse pitcher in multicolored shiny glazes, 6½" tall, Black Mark #1 (with no © Walt Disney), $75.00 – 100.00.

Plate 392. Smaller Mickey Mouse pitcher in multicolored shiny glazes, 4" tall, Black Mark #1 (with no © Walt Disney), $55.00 – 75.00.

Plate 393. Goldcastle owl pitcher in multicolored luster glazes, 4¾" Black Mark #43, $30.00 – 45.00.

Plate 394. Cat pitcher in multicolored shiny glazes, 3½" tall, Black Mark #2, $20.00 – 35.00.

Plate 395. Lidded pitcher with liner plate set decorated after the style of Clarice Cliff in multicolored shiny glazes, 8" tall, pitcher Blind Mark #1 and plate Black Mark #22, set $30.00 – 40.00.

Plate 396. (Left) Large pitcher in cream shiny glaze with black silhouettes, 5" tall, Black Mark #1, $20.00 – 30.00. (Right) Large pitcher in cream and multicolored shiny glazes, 5¾" tall, Black Mark #118, $15.00 – 25.00.

Plate 397. Tall pitcher and glass set in green and black shiny glaze, pitcher 8½" tall, all Black Mark #28, $20.00 – 35.00 with four or six mugs.

Plate 398. Goldcastle large cache pot with Dutch people in multicolored luster and shiny glazes, 5¾" tall, Blue Mark #43, $15.00 – 25.00.

Plate 399. Dutch boy cache pot in multicolored luster and shiny glazes with windmill silhouette decal, 4¼" tall, Black Mark #1, $15.00 – 25.00.

Plate 400. Dutch boy cache pot in multicolored luster glazes, 4¼" tall, Black Mark #1, $15.00 – 25.00.

Plate 401. (Left) Cherub cache pot in multicolored shiny glazes, 3¾" tall, Red Mark #2, $15.00 – 25.00. (Right) Dutch people cache pot in multicolored shiny glazes, 3¾" tall, Red Mark #1, $15.00 – 25.00.

Plate 402. Maruyama girl with basket cache pot or vase in multicolored luster glazes, the mate to plate 354B in *The Collector's Guide to Made in Japan Ceramics, Book 1*, 3¾" tall, Red Mark #65 and Blind Mark #1, $28.00 – 38.00.

Plate 403. Girl with doll buggy cache pot in multicolored luster and shiny glazes, 4" tall, Black Mark #1, $15.00 – 25.00.

Plate 404. Flower girl cache pot or vase in multicolored shiny glazes, 6½" tall, Black Mark #2, $20.00 – 30.00.

Plate 405. Clown cache pot or cigarette holder in multicolored luster and shiny glazes, 3½" tall, Black Mark #1, $25.00 – 35.00.

Plate 406. Boy with top hat and dog cache pot or toothpick holder in multicolored shiny glazes, 5½" tall, Mark #2, $15.00 – 25.00.

Plate 407. Rickshaw cache pot in multicolored shiny glazes, 3½" tall, Mark obscured, $15.00 – 25.00.

Plate 408. Indian cache pot in multicolored luster glazes, 3¼" tall, Red Mark #1, $25.00 – 35.00.

Plate 420. Hen and rooster cache pot in multicolored shiny glazes, 4½" tall, Black Mark #1, $15.00 – 25.00.

Plate 421. (Left) Duck cache pot in multicolored shiny glazes, 4½" tall, Black Mark #2, $15.00 – 25.00. (Right) Chick cache pot in multicolored shiny glazes, 5¼" tall, Green Mark #3A, $15.00 – 25.00.

Plate 422. Bird cache pot in multicolored shiny glazes, 4" tall, Black Mark #1, $15.00 – 25.00.

Plate 423. Bird cache pot in multicolored shiny glazes, 4½" tall, Black Mark #2, $15.00 – 25.00.

Plate 424. (Left) Animal cache pot or pincushion in multicolored shiny glazes, 3¼" tall, Black Mark #2, $10.00 – 15.00. (Right) Baby buggy cache pot in pink shiny glaze, 4½" tall, Black Mark #1, $10.00 – 15.00.

Plate 425. Large jardiniere with bird motif in multicolored shiny glazes, 7¼" tall, Red Mark #1, $35.00 – 50.00.

Plate 426. Cache pot in green and cream shiny glaze, 5¼" tall, Black Mark #1, $15.00 – 25.00.

Plate 427. Cache pot in green and cream shiny glaze, 4½" tall, Black Mark #1, $10.00 – 15.00.

Plate 428. (Left) Duck cache pot in multicolored shiny glazes, 3½" tall, Black Mark #1, $10.00 – 15.00. (Right) Bird cache pot in multicolored shiny glazes, 3½" tall, Black Mark #1, $10.00 – 15.00.

Plate 429. Cache pot and liner plate in multicolored luster glazes, 4¼" tall, both Black Mark #2, $15.00 – 25.00.

Plate 430. (Left) Cache pot in multicolored shiny glazes, 3¾" tall, Red Mark #2, $10.00 – 15.00. (Right) Cache pot with beer stein-style motif in multicolored shiny glazes, 3¾" tall, Black Mark #1, $15.00 – 25.00.

Plate 431. (Left) Planter in green shiny glaze, 3½" tall, Black Mark #1, $15.00 – 25.00. (Right) Planter in white shiny glaze, 3¼" tall, Black Mark #1, $10.00 – 15.00.

Plate 432. (Left) Goldcastle planter in orange shiny glaze with floral motif, 3½" tall, Red Mark #44, $15.00 – 25.00. (Right) Planter in green shiny glaze, 3¾" tall, Black Mark #1, $15.00 – 25.00.

Plate 433. Basketweave planter in pink shiny glaze with multicolored floral garland, 5½" tall, Black Mark #1, $18.00 – $28.00.

Plate 434. Goldcastle lady powder box in multicolored luster glazes, 4" tall, Black Mark #43, $65.00 – 100.00.

Plate 435. Owl powder box in multicolored luster glazes (judging from the powder and scent still inside, this one was used as a powder box for quite some time!), 4½" tall, Black Mark #56, $60.00 – 85.00.

Plate 436. Rabbit powder box in multicolored shiny glazes, 5¼" tall, Black Mark #87, $45.00 – 65.00.

Plate 437. Rabbit powder box in ivory luster glaze, 4" tall, Red Mark #99, $45.00 – 65.00.

Plate 438. Dog powder box in tan luster and multicolored shiny glazes with fruit decal, 4" tall, Red Mark #24, $25.00 – $45.00.

Plate 439. Powder box in multicolored shiny glazes with "POUDRE de GUIMET" label inside lid, 3½" tall, Black Mark #1, $20.00 – 35.00.

Plate 439a. Detail of label inside lid.

Plate 440. Powder box in multicolored semi-matte glazes with floral motif in relief, 3¾" wide, Red Mark #1, $12.00 – 20.00.

Plate 441. Bathing beauty ring tray or soap dish in multicolored luster and shiny glazes, 3½" wide, Mark #1, $35.00 – 55.00.

Plate 442. Ring tray or ash-tray in multicolored shiny glazes inscribed "Good bye sweetheart," 3½" tall, Black Mark #2, $30.00 – 45.00.

Plate 443. Bisque ring tray in multicolored shiny glazes inscribed "SOUVENIR OF BUTTE MONT," 3½" tall, Blind Mark #1, $35.00 – 50.00.

Plate 444. Ring tray in multicolored luster and shiny glazes, 4" tall, Black Mark #1 and Blind Mark #1, $25.00 – 40.00.

Plate 445. Man with a lobster on his head and a woman on his back ring tray or soap dish in multicolored matte and shiny glazes, 3¾" tall, Red Mark #1, $35.00 – 50.00.

Plate 446. Man in turban ring tray or soap dish in multicolored shiny glazes, 3¼" tall, Black Mark #1, $20.00 – 30.00.

Plate 447. Peacock ring tray or soap dish in multicolored luster and shiny glazes, 3" tall, Black Mark #79A, $25.00 – 40.00.

Plate 448. (Left) Lion ring tray or soap dish in multicolored luster and shiny glazes, 2¾" tall, Black Mark #1, $20.00 – 30.00. (Right) Man in boat ring tray or soap dish in multicolored luster and shiny glazes, 3¾" tall, Black Mark #2, $20.00 – 30.00.

Plate 449. Cat salt and pepper on pond in multi-colored shiny glazes, 5" wide, pond blue and white Label with JAPAN; salt and pepper no Mark, $20.00 – 35.00.

Plate 450. Frogs on pond salt and pepper in multi-colored shiny glazes, 5" wide, pond Black Mark #1; salt and pepper Black Mark #2, $20.00 – 35.00.

Plate 451. Three wise monkeys salt and pepper on tray inscribed "Denver, Colorado," 2¾" tall, all Black Mark #2, $25.00 – 40.00.

Plate 452. Penguin salt and pepper on tray in multicolored luster glazes, 2½" tall, Black Mark #1, $25.00 – 40.00.

Plate 453. Cat salt and pepper on tray in multicolored shiny glazes, 5" wide, tray Blue Mark #52; salt and pepper no Mark, $35.00 – 50.00.

Plate 454. Grampus salt and pepper on tray in blue and gold luster glaze, 3¼" tall, all Red Mark #1, $25.00 – 40.00.

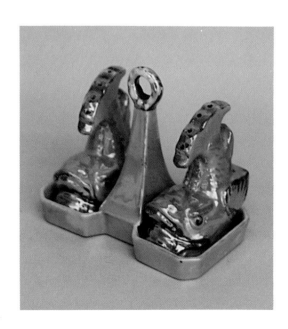

Plate 455. Elephant salt and pepper in multicolored shiny glazes, 4" tall, large elephant Black Mark #119; small one Black Mark #2, $35.00 – 50.00.

Plate 456. Rose salt and pepper on tray in multicolored luster glaze, 5¼" wide, tray Red Mark #25; salt and pepper Red Mark #2, $20.00 – 35.00.

Plate 457. Salt and pepper on tray in yellow and cobalt shiny glaze, 3½" wide, tray Blind Mark #1; salt and pepper Blind Mark #2, $15.00 – 25.00.

Plate 458. (Left) Lotus salt and pepper on tray in multicolored luster glazes, 4¼" wide, tray Red Mark #25; salt and pepper Red Mark #1, $20.00 – 30.00. (Right) Salt and pepper on tray in blue and tan luster glaze, tray Blue Mark #77; salt and pepper no Mark, $15.00 – 25.00.

Plate 459. Salt and pepper on tray in orange and black shiny glaze, 3¼" tall, $15.00 – 25.00.

Plate 460. Stacking salt and pepper in multicolored shiny glazes with label "Nanaimo Canada," both Black Mark #2, $25.00 – 40.00.

Plate 461. Asian boy and girl salt and pepper on tray in multicolored semi-matte glazes, 3¾" tall, Tray Green Mark #120; salt and pepper Green Mark #2, $25.00 – 40.00.

Plate 463. Black child with watermelon salt and pepper set, 3" tall, all Red Mark #2, $45.00 – 65.00.

Plate 462. Indian salt and pepper on tray in multicolored shiny glazes, 4" tall, Black Mark #1, $20.00 – 35.00.

Plate 464. Two salt dip and pepper shaker sets in tan and blue luster glaze (these often came three sets to a box either with all three sets the same, with each set different, or with the center set slightly different), shakers 2½" tall, all Red Mark #1, $20.00 – 30.00 per set.

Plate 465. Bird salt dip in multicolored luster and shiny glazes, 2" tall, Black Mark #52, $25.00 – 45.00.

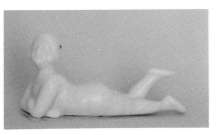

Plate 481. Naughty bathing beauty in white shiny glaze, 4" long, Blind Mark #1, $25.00 – 50.00.

Plate 482. Naughty nude ashtray in multicolored luster and shiny glazes, 3½" tall, Red Mark #12A, $35.00 – 50.00.

Plate 483. Chamber pot inscribed "ASHES" with pigs in multicolored luster and shiny glazes, 3½" tall, Mark obscured, $18.00 – 28.00.

Plate 484. (Left) Luster potty inscribed "DEAD BUTTS AND DEAD ASHES," 2½" tall, Black Mark #122, $18.00 – 28.00. (Center) Pot in white shiny glaze inscribed "REST YOUR WEARY ASH HERE," 1½" tall, no Mark, $12.00 – 18.00. (Right) Triple pot in white and tan luster glaze inscribed "Cigarettes, Matches, Ashes," 1¾" tall, Black Mark #1, $18.00 – 28.00.

Plate 485. Bisque outhouse inscribed "NEXT" with attached poem card, 3" tall, Blind Mark #2, $35.00 – 55.00.

Plate 486. Souvenir cup and saucer in blue luster glaze with multicolored decal, saucer 4" wide with Blue and Gold Label with JAPAN; cup no Mark, $2.00 – 6.00.

Plate 487. Hawaiian souvenir plate in multicolored shiny glazes, 8" wide, $25.00 – 45.00.

Plate 488. Souvenir plate in multicolored semi-matte glazes inscribed "TACOMA WASHINGTON NARROWS BRIDGE" (this was the infamous "Galloping Gertie" suspension bridge that was built in 1940, then undulated and broke apart in a windstorm four months later), 7¼" wide, Black Mark #95A, $15.00 – 25.00.

Plate 489. Souvenir plate in multicolored semi-matte glazes inscribed "CONVENTION HALL ATLANTIC CITY NJ," 5¼" wide, Red Mark #1, $5.00 – 12.00.

Plate 490. Souvenir plate in multicolored semi-matte glazes inscribed "PACIFIC OCEAN BEACH," 6" wide, Label #137, $5.00 – 12.00.

Plate 491. Souvenir plate in multicolored semi-matte glazes inscribed "UNDERWOOD PARK ON THE RED-WOOD HIGHWAY," 5¼" wide, Green Mark #123, $5.00 – 12.00.

Plate 492. Souvenir bud vase in multicolored shiny glazes with water disk inscribed "MT. RUNDLE," 3½" tall, Blue and Gold Label with JAPAN, $5.00 – 12.00.

493a. Detail of bottom of teapot inscribed "LIPTON'S TEA."

Plate 493. Noritake Lipton's individual teapot in tan luster glaze, 3¼" tall, Green Mark #53, $150.00 – 250.00.

Plate 494. Cake plate with teapot and hot water pot on tray in multicolored shiny glazes, tray 14" wide, all Red Mark #66D, set $50.00 – 75.00.

Plate 495. Teapot and hot water pot on tray in red and white shiny glaze, tray 10¾" wide, all Red Mark #47, set $45.00 – 65.00.

Plate 496. Teapot with cream, sugar, cup and saucer in multicolored semi-matte glaze with gold luster dragon motif, pot 5" tall, all Green Mark #1, set as pictured $55.00 – 65.00; $105.00 – 150.00 complete with four or six plates, cups and saucers.

Plate 497. Teapot with cream and sugar in amber mottled luster glaze, pot 4¾" tall, Black Mark #10, set $55.00 – 65.00 as pictured; $105.00 – 150.00 complete with four or six plates, cups and saucers.

Plate 498. Figural teapot with cream and sugar in multicolored shiny glazes, all Label #134, set $45.00 – 75.00.

Plate 499. Granny teapot with cream and sugar, pot 8" tall, all Black Mark #60A, set $100.00 – 125.00.

Plate 500. Meito teapot and tile in tan luster glaze with multicolored floral motif, Green and Red Mark #64, $40.00 – 65.00.

Plate 501. Teapot with airbrush motif of crows in multicolored semi-matte glazes, 5" tall, Mark #124, $40.00 – 65.00.

Plate 502. Noritake teapot in multicolored shiny glazes, 5½" tall, Green Mark #53B, $30.00 – 45.00.

Plate 503. English style teapot with windmill motif in brown shiny glaze on white body *(shown with an earthenware body in the 1933 Sears Catalog with assorted decorations for 59¢ each. Earthenware can be white as well as brown, although the white is more unusual)*, 5¼" tall, Yellow Mark #1, $20.00 – 35.00.

Plate 504. Teapot in teal luster glaze with multicolored tree and house motif, 4¾" tall, Red Mark #66, $30.00 – 45.00.

Plate 505. Meito teapot in multicolored shiny glazes with pine cones and leaves, 4¾" tall, Green and Red Mark #64, $30.00 – 45.00.

Plate 506. Teapot in white shiny glaze with multicolored airbrushed waterfall motif, 5½" tall, Red Mark #125, $30.00 – 45.00.

Plate 507. Quimper-style teapot in multicolored shiny glazes, 7¼" tall, Blind Mark #1, $45.00 – 55.00.

Plate 508. Goldcastle cat teapot in multicolored shiny glazes, 8" tall, Black Mark #43 with patent #141896 (a 1943 patent number), $45.00 – 85.00.

Plate 509. Elephant teapot in multicolored luster glazes, 5¾" tall, Red Mark #25, $45.00 – 85.00.

Plate 510. Demitasse cup and saucer set in amber and tan luster glaze on metal stand, saucers 4½" wide with Red Mark #50; cups and stand no Mark, set as pictured $50.00 – 75.00.

Plate 511. Demitasse pot in opal and tan luster glaze with pink floral motif, 7½" tall, Black Mark #1, $20.00 – 30.00.

Plate 512. Toothbrush holder in multicolored shiny glazes inscribed "THE THREE BEARS" (but it's Papa and two boys – where's Mama?), 5" tall, Black Mark #2 and Blind Mark #18, $125.00 – 150.00.

Plate 513. Animal toothbrush holder in tan luster glaze, 3¼" tall, Black Mark #1, $85.00 – 125.00.

Plate 514. Donkey toothbrush holder inscribed "If tail is dry–fine. If tail is wet–rain. If tail moves–windy. If tail cannot be seen–fog. If tail is frozen–cold. If tail falls out–earthquake," in multicolored shiny glazes *(shown in the 1933 Sears catalog as a "Novelty Donkey Joker Barometer, Hangs on Wall, Can be used as Tooth Brush Holder," for 10¢)*, 8½" long, Black Mark #1, $20.00 – 40.00.

Plate 515. Dutch girl toothbrush holder in multicolored shiny glazes, 5¼" tall, Blind Mark #1, $85.00 – 125.00.

Plate 516. Maruyama clown with blue mustache toothbrush holder in multicolored shiny glazes, 5" tall, Blind Mark #65, $85.00 – 125.00.

Plate 517. Goldcastle clown toothbrush holder in multicolored shiny glazes, 5½" tall, Red Mark #43, $85.00 – 125.00.

Plate 518. Orphan Annie and Sandy bisque toothbrush holder in multicolored semi-matte glazes, 4" tall, Black Mark #2 and © FAS S1565, $125.00 – 175.00.

Plate 519. Moon Mullins and Kayo bisque toothbrush holder in multicolored semi-matte glazes, 3¾" tall, Black Mark #2 and Blind Mark #1 and © FAS S1563, $125.00 – 175.00.

Plate 520. Camera boy tooth-pick holder or cache pot in multicolored shiny glazes, 3½" tall, Black Mark #1, $20.00 – $35.00.

Plate 521. Bisque Asian figure toothpick holder in multicol-ored matte glazes, 3½" tall, Mark #2, $20.00 – 35.00.

Plate 522. Asian lady head toothpick holder in multicolored shiny glazes with tan luster interior, 3¼" tall, Red Mark #25, $20.00 – 35.00.

Plate 523. Asparagus tray in multicolored luster glazes, 10¾" long, Red Mark #1, $30.00 – 45.00.

Plate 524. Bank in multicolored shiny glazes from the Pixie Kitchen, a restaurant in Oceanlake, Oregon, which has been closed for many years (the label on the box has the pre-zip postal code on it, which means at least the label was printed prior to 1963), 4½" tall, Label #138, $15.00 – 25.00.

Plate 525. Basket in blue shiny glaze, 4" tall, Black Mark #1, $12.00 – 18.00.

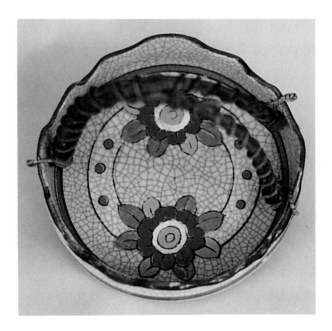

Plate 526. Rustic basket in multicolored cream crackle and semi-matte glazes, 7¼" wide, Red Mark #25, $25.00 – 45.00.

Plate 527. Berry bowl set in multicolored luster and shiny glazes, master bowl 8½" wide with Red Mark #74; small bowls no Mark, set $20.00 – 35.00.

Plate 528. Meito scenic cake plate in multicolored shiny glazes, 9½" wide, Red and Green Mark #64, $10.00 – 20.00.

Plate 529. Elephant perpetual calendar holder in multicolored shiny glazes, 2¾" tall, Black Mark #2 and Blind Mark #2, $25.00 – 35.00 as pictured ($35.00 – 55.00 if complete with calendar pages).

Plate 530. Large colonial gentleman perpetual calendar in multicolored luster and shiny glazes, 5½" wide, Black Mark #126, $35.00 – 55.00.

Plate 531. Duck candy or tobacco jar in tan luster and multicolored shiny glazes, 4¾" tall, $60.00 – 85.00.

Plate 532. Covered casserole bowl in multicolored shiny glazes with flower finial, 10" wide, Black Mark #1 and Blind Mark #76, $20.00 – 35.00.

Plate 533. Covered casserole bowl in multicolored shiny glazes with strawberry finial, 7½" wide, Black Mark #1, $20.00 – 35.00.

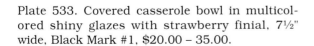

Plate 534. Individual covered casserole bowl in the form of a koi in orange shiny glaze (similar to a Czech set, which has a large covered koi casserole and six or eight individual covered koi bowls) 5¾" long, Red Mark #24, $20.00 – 35.00.

Plate 535. Noritake celery tray with poppy motif in multicolored luster and semi-matte glazes, 13¼" long, Blue Mark #26, $50.00 – 65.00.

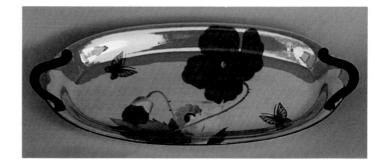

Plate 536. Noritake celery tray and salt dip set in multicolored luster glazes, tray 12" long, all Green Mark #53, set $55.00 – 85.00.

Plate 537. Clothes brush in multicolored shiny glazes, 5" tall, Red Mark #1, $35.00 – 55.00.

Plate 538. Noritake condensed milk can holder in blue and multicolored luster glazes, 5½" tall, Red Mark #26, $50.00-$75.00 as pictured ($75.00 – 125.00 with liner plate).

Plate 539. Noritake condensed milk can holder in teal and multicolored luster glazes, 5½" tall, Red Mark #26, $50.00 – 75.00 as pictured ($75.00 – 125.00 with liner plate).

Plate 539a. Picture of the finger hole in the base of a condensed milk can holder. The hole enabled one to push up an open can to pour from it or to remove it without spilling the milk.

Plate 540. Divided relish dish in cream crackle glaze with multicolored floral motif, 8¼" wide, Black Mark #50, $18.00 – 28.00.

Plate 541. Chick egg cup in black and multicolored shiny glazes, 3" tall, Red Mark #24, $20.00 – 30.00.

Plate 542. Hen egg cup in multicolored luster and shiny glazes, 3¼" tall, Black Mark #1, $20.00 – 30.00.

Plate 543. Rooster egg cup in multicolored luster and shiny glazes, 3" tall, Black Mark #1, $20.00 – 30.00.

Plate 544. Joséf Original egg separator in yellow and multicolored shiny glazes, 4" tall, Label #69, $25.00 – 35.00.

Plate 545. Hatpin holder or bud vase in amber luster with multicolored floral motif, 4¾" tall, Red Mark #1, $20.00 – 35.00.

Plate 546. Apple knife holder in multicolored shiny glazes, 3¼" tall, Black Mark #2, $25.00 – 45.00.

Plate 547. Oil lamp with cat on books in multicolored shiny glazes, 5¾" tall, Black and White label with JAPAN, $15.00 – 25.00.

Plate 548. Ovoid mayonnaise set in tan luster and green and multicolored luster and shiny glazes, plate 7¼" wide, bowl and plate Black Mark #21A, $35.00 – 65.00.

Plate 549. Noritake mayonnaise set in multicolored luster glazes, plate 6" wide with no Mark; bowl and ladle Green Mark #53, $50.00 – 75.00.

Plate 550. Elephant mug in blue and gray crackle glaze, 3½" tall, purchased new in 1969, no Mark (original label has been washed off), $2.00 – 5.00.

Plate 551. Paperweight with sleeping Mexican in multicolored shiny glazes, 5½" long, Black Mark #2, $20.00 – 35.00.

Plate 552. Flower place card holders in multicolored shiny glazes, 2" tall, all Red Mark #2, $30.00 – 40.00 each.

Plate 553. Colonial lady place card holder in multicolored shiny glazes, 2¾" tall, Red Mark #1, $35.00 – 50.00.

Plate 554. Bird pomander in multicolored shiny glazes, 4½" tall, Black Mark #2, $25.00 – 40.00.

Plate 555. Range set in multicolored shiny glazes, 5" tall, all Black Mark #62, set $45.00 – 75.00.

Plate 556. Cat reamer in multicolored luster and shiny glazes with label "TORONTO EXHIBITION," 3½" tall, Black Mark #2, $75.00 – 125.00.

Plate 557. Salt box in multicolored shiny glazes, 5½" tall, Black Mark #1, $50.00 – 70.00.

Plate 558. Noritake sandwich server in multicolored luster glazes, 7¾" wide, Red Mark #53, $30.00 – 50.00.

Plate 559. Snack set in multicolored luster and shiny glazes (these were also sold as sandwich sets, toast sets, and much later as TV sets), tray 8" wide with Black Mark #1; cup no Mark, $15.00 – 25.00.

Plate 560. Noritake snack set in multicolored shiny glazes, tray 8½" wide, both pieces Green Mark #53, $15.00 – 25.00.

Plate 561. Sweetmeat dish set in teal luster glaze with white floral motif in lacquer presentation box (these sets were made in different diameters and many different motifs, but usually the motif on the dishes echoes an element of the motif on the box), 10" in diameter, dishes all Red Mark #66; box Mark #1, $75.00 – 95.00.

Plate 562. Toast rack in blue and tan luster glaze, 5½" long, Black Mark #1, $25.00 – 50.00.

Plate 561a. Detail of cover of sweetmeat presentation box.

Plate 563. Toast rack with fruit motif in multicolored luster and shiny glazes, 6½" long, Black Mark #1, $25.00 – 50.00.

Plate 564. "Hummel-style" wall plaque signed "Norton" in multicolored semi – matte glazes, 5" tall, Silver label with Mark #7 with different numbers (SH71B32) and no date, $15.00 – 25.00.

Plate 565. Animal wall plaques in multicolored shiny glazes, 5¼" to 5½" wide, all Green Mark #1, $15.00 – 20.00 each.

Plate 566. Kinkozan water jug in multicolored shiny glazes *(a pre-World War II piece from the Akiyama store)*, 6¼" tall, Red Mark #49, $15.00 – 25.00 as pictured ($55.00 – 80.00 if complete with matching water glass).

Plate 567. Water set in multicolored luster and shiny glazes, 7¼" tall, jug no Mark; glass Mark obscured, $55.00 – 85.00.

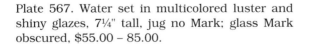

Plate 568. Dog vase in multicolored luster glazes, 5" tall, Black Mark #1, $45.00 – 70.00.

Plate 569. Bird vase in multicolored luster and shiny glazes, 6¼" tall, Black Mark #1, $45.00 – 70.00.

Plate 570. Bird vase in multicolored luster and shiny glazes *(shown in the 1931 – 32 Fall-Winter Sears catalog for 49¢, then in the 1932 Spring catalog for 39¢),* 7¼" tall, Red Mark #24, $35.00 – 50.00.

Plate 571. Bird vase in multicolored luster and shiny glazes, 5" tall, Black Mark #1, $35.00 – 50.00.

Plate 572. Vase in tan luster glaze with multi-colored bird molded in relief, 6" tall, Black Mark #1, $35.00 – 50.00.

Plate 573. Bird vase in multicol-ored shiny glazes, 4" tall, Blind Mark #1, $20.00 – 30.00.

Plate 574. Frog and apple vase in multi-colored shiny glazes, 4½" tall, Green Mark #68, $20.00 – 35.00.

Plate 575. Carp vase in white shiny glaze, 3½" tall, Black Mark #2, $5.00 – 12.00.

Plate 576. Carp trio vase in celadon glaze, 7¼" tall, Black Mark #1, $30.00 – 60.00.

Plate 577. Swan vase in white luster glaze, 5" tall, Black Mark #18, $20.00 – 30.00.

Plate 578. (Left) Man with cane vase in multicolored shiny glazes, 5½" tall, Black Mark #111A, $20.00 – 30.00. (Right) Dog vase in multicolored shiny glazes, 3¼" tall, Black Mark #1, $20.00 – 30.00.

Plate 579. (Left) Cowboy vase in multicolored shiny glazes, 2¾" tall, Mark obscured, $20.00 – 30.00. (Right) Clown and dog vase in multicolored luster and shiny glazes, 2½" tall, Black Mark #2, $20.00 – 30.00.

Plate 580. Angel mini vase in multicolored shiny glazes, 3½" tall, Red Mark #23, $16.00 – 22.00.

Plate 581. Mary and Jesus vase in multicolored shiny glazes, 9" tall, Label #139, $18.00 – 28.00.

Plate 582. Dancing girl vase in multicolored shiny glazes, 4" tall, Black Mark #127, $15.00 – 25.00.

Plate 583. Girl skirtholder vase in blue and white shiny glaze, 7¼" tall, Black Mark #1, $15.00 – 25.00.

Plate 584. Dutch girl vase in multicolored shiny glazes, 6½" tall, Black Mark #1, $20.00 – 40.00.

Plate 585. Moon and cherub vase in blue and yellow shiny glaze, 5" tall, Mark #1, $20.00 – 30.00.

Plate 586. Watering can vase in green glaze with multicolored house motif, 5¼" tall, Red Mark #24, $12.00 – 20.00.

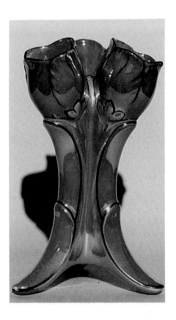

Plate 587. Triple tulip vase in multicolored luster glazes, 6" tall, Green Mark #1, $50.00 – 65.00.

Plate 588. Triple flower-form vase in green shiny glaze, 8½" tall, Black Mark #1, $15.00 – 25.00.

Plate 589. Kinkozan vase in black and orange semi-matte glaze, 7½" tall, Red Mark #49, $85.00 – 135.00.

Plate 590. Kinkozan vase with bird motif in multicolored semi-matte glazes, 9½" tall, Red Mark #49, $85.00 – 135.00.

Plate 591. (Left) Vase in tan luster and multicolored shiny glazes, 4½" tall, Black Mark #1, $20.00 – 35.00. (Right) Vase with flower frog in amber luster and multicolored shiny glazes, 5½" tall, vase Red Mark #1; frog no Mark, $35.00 – 55.00.

Plate 592. (Left and Right) Pair of vases in orange shiny glaze with moriage dragon motif, 4" tall, both Red Mark #1, $15.00 – 25.00 each. (Center) Vase in orange shiny glaze with white floral motif, 6¾" tall, Black Mark #1, $20.00 – $40.00.

Plate 593. Vase in gold shiny glaze with opal luster interior, 7¼" tall, Red Mark #32, $28.00 – 40.00.

Plate 594. Three-part vase with floral motif in white shiny glaze, 5½" tall, Black Mark #1, $10.00 – 20.00.

Plate 595. Bud vase in multicolored luster glazes with green giraffe (with humps!), 5¼" tall, Black Mark #1, $15.00 – $25.00.

Plate 596. Vase with bird motif (could be made into a lamp because it has a dimple but no cord hole), in multicolored shiny glazes, 6¼" tall, Black Mark #1, $25.00 – 40.00.

Plate 597. Vase in blue luster and multicolored shiny glazes (could be made into a lamp because it has a dimple but no cord hole), 6" tall, Red Mark #1, $25.00 – 40.00.

Plate 598. Vase in white shiny glaze with multicolored sponged and floral motif, 7½" tall, Red Mark #25, $20.00 – 35.00.

Plate 599. Folk art pottery diamond point vase in blue and brown shiny glaze, 5¼" tall, Black Mark #1, $25.00 – 35.00.

Plate 600. Rustic vase in cream crackle glaze with multicolored bird motif, 6½" tall, Red Mark #1, $25.00 – 45.00.

Plate 601. Tall vase in cream crackle glaze with multicolored leaf motif, 9¾" tall, Black Mark #128, $25.00 – 45.00.

Plate 602. Vase of recent manufacture in multicolored shiny glazes with multicolored bird motif, 6½" tall, Gold Label with JAPAN, $12.00 – 20.00.

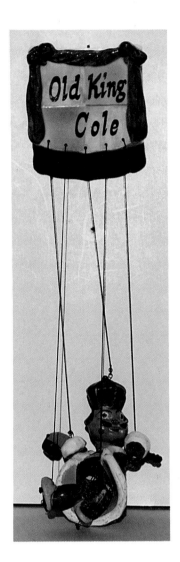

Plate 603. Old King Cole wall pocket in multicolored shiny glazes, 12½" long, Label #140,
$100.00 – 150.00.

Plate 604. Indian head wall pocket
in multicolored luster and shiny
glazes, 7¼" long, Black Mark #1,
$45.00 – 75.00.

Plate 605. Mini lady head wall pocket in multicolored shiny glazes, 3" long, Red Mark #129,
$25.00 – 40.00.

Plate 606. Skirtholder lady wall pocket in multi-colored luster and shiny glazes, 5¼" long, Red Mark #18 and Blind Mark #18, $20.00 – 35.00.

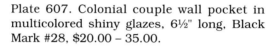

Plate 607. Colonial couple wall pocket in multicolored shiny glazes, 6½" long, Black Mark #28, $20.00 – 35.00.

Plate 608. Colonial lady wall pocket in multicolored luster and shiny glazes, 6½" long, Black Mark #1, $25.00 – 40.00.

Plate 609. Girl with lute and roses wall pocket in multicolored luster and shiny glazes, 6" long, Black Mark #1, $20.00 – 35.00.

Plate 610. Girl and doll buggy wall pocket in multicolored shiny glazes, 5½" tall, Red Mark #2, $22.00 – 30.00.

Plate 611. Sailboat wall pocket in multicolored luster and shiny glazes, 5¼" long, Blind Mark #2, $30.00 – 45.00.

Plate 612. Floral wall pocket in multicolored luster and shiny glazes, 7½" long, Red Mark #56, $40.00 – 60.00.

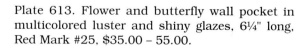

Plate 613. Flower and butterfly wall pocket in multicolored luster and shiny glazes, 6¼" long, Red Mark #25, $35.00 – 55.00.

Plate 614. Basket-handled floral wall pocket in multicolored luster and shiny glazes, 7½" long, Red Mark #20, $25.00 – 40.00.

Plate 615. Basketweave wall pocket in cream shiny glaze with multicolored floral motif, 6¼" long, Black Mark #130, $20.00 – 35.00.

Plate 616. Carrot wall pocket in green and orange shiny glaze, 5½" long, Black Mark #2, $20.00 – 35.00.

Plate 617. Bird on flower pot wall pocket in multicolored luster and shiny glazes, 6¾" long, Red Mark #20, $35.00 – 55.00.

Plate 618. Bird wall pocket in multicolored luster glazes, 7" long, Black Mark #66A, $40.00 – 60.00.

Plate 619. Large bird wall pocket in multicolored luster and shiny glazes, 9¼" long, Green Mark #25, $45.00 – 65.00.

Plate 620. Figural bird and flower wall pocket in multicolored luster and shiny glazes, 6½" long, Red Mark #20, $40.00 – 60.00.

Plate 621. Bird wall pocket in blue and white shiny glaze, 6½" long, Black Mark #1, $20.00 – 30.00.

Plate 622. Flamingo wall pocket in multicolored shiny glazes, 6½" long, Green Mark #107, $25.00 – 35.00.

Plate 623. Duck figural wall pocket in multicolored shiny glazes on wire frame, 8¼" tall, Black Mark #1, $20.00 – 35.00.

Plate 624. Polar bear wall pocket in multicolored luster and shiny glazes, 5½" long, Red Mark #2, $22.00 – 30.00.

Plate 625. Scottie wall pocket in multicolored shiny glazes, 5" long, Mark obscured, $28.00 – 38.00.

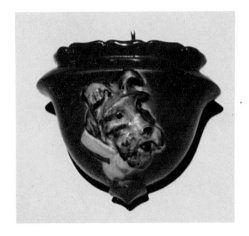

Plate 626. Scottie wall pocket in multicolored shiny glazes, 3½" long, Red Mark #1, $25.00 – 40.00.

Plate 627. Doggie wall pocket in multicolored shiny glazes, 3¾" long, Black Mark #38A, $25.00 – 35.00.

Plate 628. Wall pocket (after a style of American art pottery) in multicolored shiny glazes, 7" long, Black Mark #1, $20.00 – 35.00.

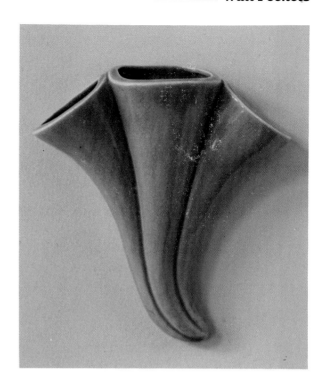

Plate 629. Tri-part wall pocket in pink shiny glaze, 7¾" long, Black Mark #1, $15.00 – 25.00.

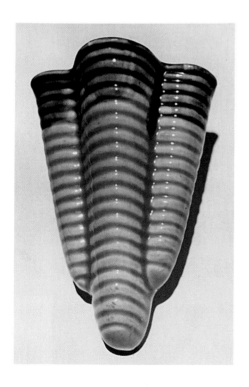

Plate 630. Corner wall pocket (the back is triangular to fit into a corner) in tan and blue shiny glaze, 6" long, Black Mark #1, $25.00 – 35.00.

Plate 631. Pitcher-shaped wall pocket in multicolored shiny glazes, 6¾" long, Black Mark #1, $20.00 – 35.00.

Plate 640. Wall pocket with flower and butterfly motif in multicolored shiny glazes with gold luster rim, 7" long, Black Mark #1, $35.00 – 50.00.

Plate 641. Wall pocket in multicolored shiny glazes, 7¼" long, Red Mark #28, $30.00 – 40.00.

Plate 642. Goldcastle wall pocket in multicolored shiny glazes, 9" long, Red Mark #43, $25.00 – 40.00.

Plate 628. Wall pocket (after a style of American art pottery) in multicolored shiny glazes, 7" long, Black Mark #1, $20.00 – 35.00.

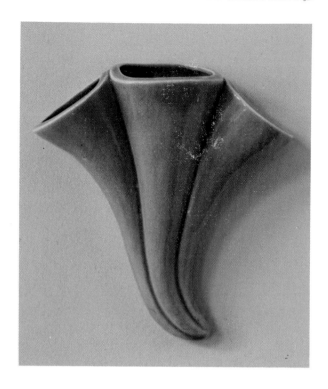

Plate 629. Tri-part wall pocket in pink shiny glaze, 7¾" long, Black Mark #1, $15.00 – 25.00.

Plate 630. Corner wall pocket (the back is triangular to fit into a corner) in tan and blue shiny glaze, 6" long, Black Mark #1, $25.00 – 35.00.

Plate 631. Pitcher-shaped wall pocket in multicolored shiny glazes, 6¾" long, Black Mark #1, $20.00 – 35.00.

Plate 632. Wall pocket in multicolored luster glazes with moriage bird
motif, 7½" long, Red Mark #28,
$45.00 – 65.00.

Plate 633. Wall pocket in multicolored luster glazes with moriage bird
and rosebud motif, 6¼" long, Red
Mark #28, $40.00 – 60.00.

Plate 634. Wall pocket in multicolored
luster glazes with moriage bird and
branch motif, 6¼" long, Red Mark #28,
$40.00 – 60.00.

Plate 635. Wall pocket in gray semi-
matte glaze with moriage dragon
motif, 7½" long, Red and Black
Mark #131, $30.00 – 45.00.

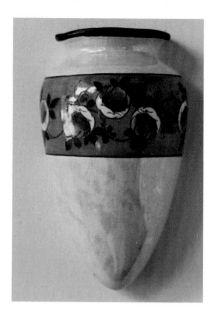

Plate 636. Wall pocket with floral band in multicolored luster glazes, 7¼" long, Green Mark #20, $30.00 – 45.00.

Plate 637. Flower and butterfly wall pocket in multicolored luster glazes, 8½" long, Red Mark #20, $40.00 – 60.00.

Plate 638. Goldcastle wall pocket in multicolored shiny glazes, 8½" long, Red Mark #43, $40.00 – 60.00.

Plate 639. Wall pocket in tan luster with orange and yellow floral motif, 5½" long, Black Mark #1, $30.00 – 45.00.

Plate 640. Wall pocket with flower and butterfly motif in multicolored shiny glazes with gold luster rim, 7" long, Black Mark #1, $35.00 – 50.00.

Plate 641. Wall pocket in multicolored shiny glazes, 7¼" long, Red Mark #28, $30.00 – 40.00.

Plate 642. Goldcastle wall pocket in multicolored shiny glazes, 9" long, Red Mark #43, $25.00 – 40.00.

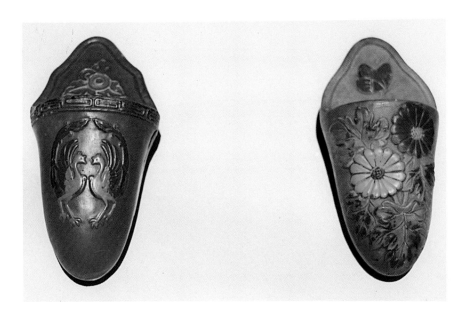

Plate 643. Chalkware wall pockets in multicolored semi-matte glazes, 6½" long, both Blind Mark #3 with NAME WARE, $20.00 – 30.00 each.

Plate 644. Long Tokan-abe-type wall pocket in multicolored matte glazes, 9¼" long, Blind Mark #1, $20.00 – 30.00.

Plate 645. The granddaddy of all wall pockets! Huge Tokanabe-type wall pocket in multicolored semi-matte glazes, 10" long and weighing in at around two pounds, Blind Mark #1, $20.00 – 35.00.

Plate 646. Metal postal scale and stamp dispenser, 4¼" wide, Gold and Red label with JAPAN, $15.00 – 20.00.

Plate 647. Composition dog bank, 5¾" tall, Mark #8A with number M-6915, $15.00 – 25.00.

⚐ **CLEANING TIPS** ⚐

Neal Skibinski passed along a suggestion. He purchased the lovely marbled amber luster teapot, cream and sugar set in Plate 497, but the cream pitcher had been abused and had a very dull and crusted exterior, which hand washing did not improve. He lightly used Wenol, a fine German silver polish, and the luster polished right up, as you can see. He also suggested another German polish, Simichrome. These are available through jewelry stores, silver departments, or antique stores.

Am I suggesting that you try silver polish on all your luster pieces? NO, and especially not on the pieces with thin luster. However, if a piece is so badly corroded that it's virtually a lost cause, you might want to risk trying a really good polish (not the grocery store kind) on a tiny, unobtrusive spot to see if it can be restored. After all, luster is made from metal salts, so it is logical that silver polish would make it shine.

Prices are w
item or per

There are large vases currently being imported from China that look very much like Hand Painted Nippon or early Made in Japan. The motifs and glaze quality are pretty decent, so it would be easy to confuse them with authentic early Japanese ware. They should have a small, oval paper label that says MADE IN CHINA on the base, but it is not very sticky and falls off easily. We bought these two vases to photograph for this book at a flea market for $15.00 each in 1996. There were more than a dozen different motifs, all on the same blank.

The ways to differentiate them from old Japanese vases are the quality of the base, the size, and shape. As you can see, there is a lot of frit and roughness on the base which the glaze does not completely cover. Made in Japan vases are usually more finished. This is also not a common size or shape for Made in Japan vases.

Plate 648. Chinese vase in multicolored shiny glazes, 13" tall, no Mark, $15.00 – 25.00.

Selections from 1960s Pacific Orient Imports catalog

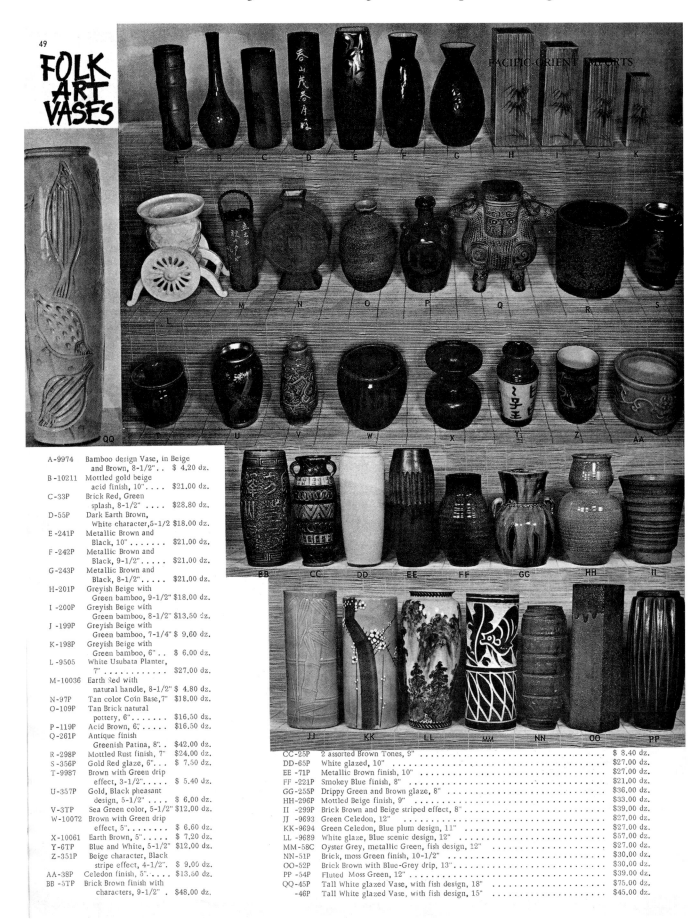

49

FOLK ART VASES

PACIFIC-ORIENT IMPORTS

A-9974	Bamboo design Vase, in Beige and Brown, 8-1/2"..	$ 4.20 dz.
B-10211	Mottled gold beige acid finish, 10"....	$21.00 dz.
C-33P	Brick Red, Green splash, 8-1/2"	$28.80 dz.
D-55P	Dark Earth Brown, White character, 5-1/2	$18.00 dz.
E-241P	Metallic Brown and Black, 10"	$21.00 dz.
F-242P	Metallic Brown and Black, 9-1/2".....	$21.00 dz.
G-243P	Metallic Brown and Black, 8-1/2"....	$21.00 dz.
H-201P	Greyish Beige with Green bamboo, 9-1/2"	$18.00 dz.
I-200P	Greyish Beige with Green bamboo, 8-1/2"	$13.50 dz.
J-199P	Greyish Beige with Green bamboo, 7-1/4"	$ 9.60 dz.
K-198P	Greyish Beige with Green bamboo, 6"..	$ 6.00 dz.
L-9505	White Usubata Planter, 7"	$27.00 dz.
M-10036	Earth Red with natural handle, 8-1/2"	$ 4.80 dz.
N-97P	Tan color Coin Base, 7"	$18.00 dz.
O-109P	Tan Brick natural pottery, 6"......	$16.50 dz.
P-119P	Acid Brown, 6".....	$16.50 dz.
Q-261P	Antique finish Greenish Patina, 8"..	$42.00 dz.
R-298P	Mottled Rust finish, 7"	$24.00 dz.
S-356P	Gold Red glaze, 6"...	$ 7.50 dz.
T-9987	Brown with Green drip effect, 3-1/2".....	$ 5.40 dz.
U-357P	Gold, Black pheasant design, 5-1/2"	$ 6.00 dz.
V-3TP	Sea Green color, 5-1/2"	$12.00 dz.
W-10072	Brown with Green drip effect, 5".....	$ 6.60 dz.
X-10061	Earth Brown, 5".....	$ 7.20 dz.
Y-6TP	Blue and White, 5-1/2"	$12.00 dz.
Z-351P	Beige character, Black stripe effect, 4-1/2"	$ 9.00 dz.
AA-38P	Celedon finish, 5"....	$13.50 dz.
BB-5TP	Brick Brown finish with characters, 9-1/2"	$48.00 dz.

CC-25P	2 assorted Brown Tones, 9"	....	$ 8.40 dz.
DD-65P	White glazed, 10"	....	$27.00 dz.
EE-71P	Metallic Brown finish, 10"	....	$27.00 dz.
FF-221P	Smokey Blue finish, 8"	....	$21.00 dz.
GG-255P	Drippy Green and Brown glaze, 8"	....	$36.00 dz.
HH-296P	Mottled Beige finish, 9"	....	$33.00 dz.
II-299P	Brick Brown and Beige striped effect, 8"	....	$39.00 dz.
JJ-9693	Green Celedon, 12"	....	$27.00 dz.
KK-9694	Green Celedon, Blue plum design, 11"	....	$27.00 dz.
LL-9689	White glaze, Blue scenic design, 12"	....	$57.00 dz.
MM-58C	Oyster Grey, metallic Green, fish design, 12"	....	$27.00 dz.
NN-51P	Brick, moss Green finish, 10-1/2"	....	$30.00 dz.
OO-52P	Brick Brown with Blue-Grey drip, 13"	....	$30.00 dz.
PP-54P	Fluted Moss Green, 12"	....	$39.00 dz.
QQ-45P	Tall White glazed Vase, with fish design, 18"	....	$75.00 dz.
-46P	Tall White glazed Vase, with fish design, 15"	....	$45.00 dz.

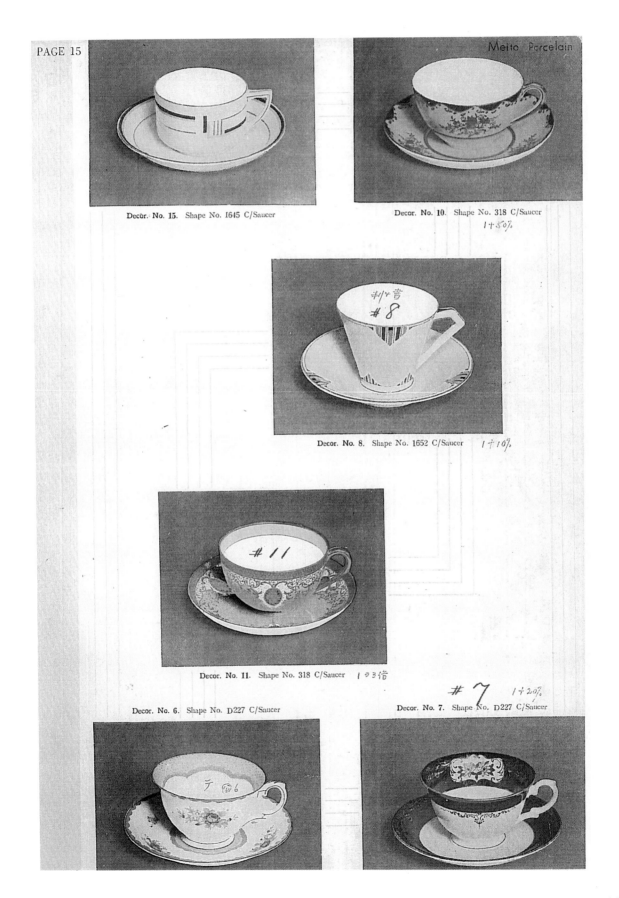

PAGE 15

Meito Porcelain

Decor. No. 15. Shape No. 1645 C/Saucer

Decor. No. 10. Shape No. 318 C/Saucer
1+50%

#8

Decor. No. 8. Shape No. 1652 C/Saucer 1+10%

#11

Decor. No. 11. Shape No. 318 C/Saucer 1ヶ3倍

#7 1+20%

Decor. No. 6. Shape No. D227 C/Saucer

Decor. No. 7. Shape No. D227 C/Saucer

Selections from a 1940 Meito China Company catalog

Decor. No. 47.   Shape No. 318 C/Saucer

Decor. No. 51.   Shape No. 318 C/Saucer

Decor. No. 48.   Shape No. 318 C/Saucer

Decor. No. 52.   Shape No. 318 C/Saucer

Decor. No. 49.   Shape No. 318 C/Saucer

Decor. No. 53.   Shape No. N707 C/Saucer

Mitsui Bussan Kaisha, Ltd., Nagoya

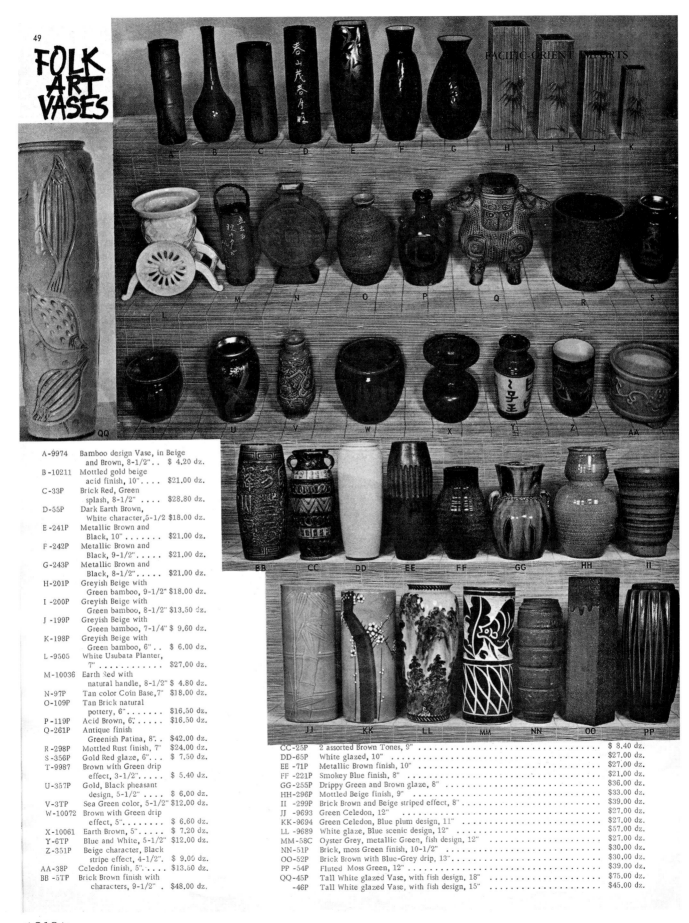

FOLK ART VASES

49

PACIFIC ORIENT IMPORTS

A-9974	Bamboo design Vase, in Beige and Brown, 8-1/2".. $ 4.20 dz.
B-10211	Mottled gold beige acid finish, 10".... $21.00 dz.
C-33P	Brick Red, Green splash, 8-1/2" .... $28.80 dz.
D-55P	Dark Earth Brown, White character, 5-1/2 $18.00 dz.
E-241P	Metallic Brown and Black, 10"...... $21.00 dz.
F-242P	Metallic Brown and Black, 9-1/2"..... $21.00 dz.
G-243P	Metallic Brown and Black, 8-1/2"..... $21.00 dz.
H-201P	Greyish Beige with Green bamboo, 9-1/2" $18.00 dz.
I-200P	Greyish Beige with Green bamboo, 8-1/2" $13.50 dz.
J-199P	Greyish Beige with Green bamboo, 7-1/4" $ 9.60 dz.
K-198P	Greyish Beige with Green bamboo, 6".. $ 6.00 dz.
L-9505	White Usubata Planter, 7"............ $27.00 dz.
M-10036	Earth Red with natural handle, 8-1/2" $ 4.80 dz.
N-97P	Tan color Coin Base, 7" $18.00 dz.
O-109P	Tan Brick natural pottery, 6"...... $16.50 dz.
P-119P	Acid Brown, 6"..... $16.50 dz.
Q-261P	Antique finish Greenish Patina, 8".. $42.00 dz.
R-298P	Mottled Rust finish, 7" $24.00 dz.
S-356P	Gold Red glaze, 6"... $ 7.50 dz.
T-9987	Brown with Green drip effect, 3-1/2"..... $ 5.40 dz.
U-357P	Gold, Black pheasant design, 5-1/2" $ 6.00 dz.
V-3TP	Sea Green color, 5-1/2" $12.00 dz.
W-10072	Brown with Green drip effect, 5"..... $ 6.60 dz.
X-10061	Earth Brown, 5"..... $ 7.20 dz.
Y-6TP	Blue and White, 5-1/2" $12.00 dz.
Z-351P	Beige character, Black stripe effect, 4-1/2" $ 9.00 dz.
AA-38P	Celedon finish, 5".... $13.50 dz.
BB-5TP	Brick Brown finish with characters, 9-1/2" . $48.00 dz.

CC-25P	2 assorted Brown Tones, 9"	$ 8.40 dz.
DD-65P	White glazed, 10"	$27.00 dz.
EE-71P	Metallic Brown finish, 10"	$27.00 dz.
FF-221P	Smokey Blue finish, 8"	$21.00 dz.
GG-255P	Drippy Green and Brown glaze, 8"	$36.00 dz.
HH-296P	Mottled Beige finish, 9"	$33.00 dz.
II-299P	Brick Brown and Beige striped effect, 8"	$39.00 dz.
JJ-9693	Green Celedon, 12"	$27.00 dz.
KK-9694	Green Celedon, Blue plum design, 11"	$27.00 dz.
LL-9689	White glaze, Blue scenic design, 12"	$57.00 dz.
MM-58C	Oyster Grey, metallic Green, fish design, 12"	$27.00 dz.
NN-51P	Brick, moss Green finish, 10-1/2"	$30.00 dz.
OO-52P	Brick Brown with Blue-Grey drip, 13"	$30.00 dz.
PP-54P	Fluted Moss Green, 12"	$39.00 dz.
QQ-45P	Tall White glazed Vase, with fish design, 18"	$75.00 dz.
-46P	Tall White glazed Vase, with fish design, 15"	$45.00 dz.

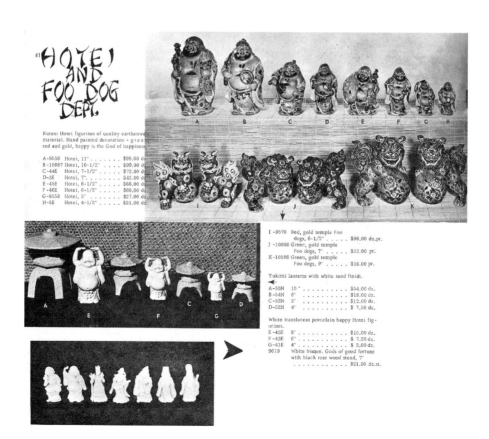

E-921 2 asst. 72.00   E-919 42.00   E-908 18.00   E-917 42.00   E-921 2 asst. 72.00

-918 30.00   E-834 12.00   GD-28 30.00 dz. pr.   E-929 3 asst. 4.80   E-927 16.50   E-922 2 asst. 24.00

B-149 60.00   B-319 36.00

E-920 30.00   A-164 24.00 dz. pr.   E-907 7.20   A-159 45.00 dz. pr.   E-928 6.60   J-852 42.00   T-157 10.20

NORCREST ANIMALS ARE GUARANTEED BEST SELLERS

A-138 8.40   A-145 2 asst. 7.20   A-158 2 asst. 7.20   A-165 2 asst. 10.50   A-133 27.00   A-134 27.00

A-146 2 asst. 7.20   A-127 6 asst. 9.00   A-141 4 asst. 21.00

A-135 21.00   A-150 24.00   A-151 36.00 dz. pr.   A-149 3 asst. 6.60   A-130 30.00

AND COLOR

A-835 24.00 dz. pr. A-527 24.00 dz. pr. A-759 48.00 dz. pr. A-883 15.00 dz. pr.

A-648 15.00 dz. pr. A-758 16.50 dz. pr. A-364 18.00 dz. pr. A-89 15.00

A-53 15.00 dz. pr. A-696 15.00 dz. pr. A-902 15.00 dz. A-884 9.00 dz. pr. A-823 72.00 dz. pr.

F-732 12 asst. 7.20 dz. F-533 12 asst. 5.40 dz. F-754 12 asst. 6.00 dz. F-969 12 asst. 6.60 dz.

BISQUE ANGEL FIGURINES

F-39 2 asst. 13.50 dz. F-934 3 asst. 9.60 dz. F-644 19.50 dz. pr. F-717 4 asst. 6.00 dz. F-987 2 asst. 10.20 dz.

F-940 9.00 dz. F-9 2 asst. 5.40 dz. F-962 3 asst. 2.40 dz. F-715 15.00 dz. pr. F-859 4 asst. 7.80 dz. F-891 4 asst. 4.80 dz.
3 asst.

F-4 2 asst. 5.40 dz. F-466 4 asst. 3.60 dz. F-6 3 asst. 5.40 dz. F-878 3 asst. 4.80 dz.

F-855 6 asst. 2.70 dz. F-881 3 asst. 3.90 dz. F-705 6 asst. 2.40 dz. F-743 3 asst. 2.10 dz. F-690 4 asst. 2.40 dz. F-897 3 asst. 9.00 dz.

F-417 6 asst. 3.60 dz. F-5 3 asst. 6.00 dz. F-807 4 asst. 3.00 dz. F-668 3 asst. 2.40 dz. F-980 3 asst. 3.90 F-921 3 asst. 3.60 dz.

F-746 4 asst. 4.80 dz. F-786 4 asst. 2.40 dz. F-882 3 asst. 4.20 dz. F-872 4 asst. 3.60 dz. F-963 3 asst. 3.60 dz.

All prices are wholesale and in dozen lots

ALPINE CHILDREN AND BABY FIGURINES

-752 10.80 dz. F-799 2 asst. 36.00 dz. F-975 6 asst. 7.20 dz. F-976 6 asst. 7.20 dz. F-628 72.00 dz. pr.

F-974 7.50 dz. F-705 6.60 dz. pr. F-37 2 asst. 10.20 dz. F-360 3 asst. 7.20 dz. F-920 3 asst. 6.00 dz. F-810 3 asst. 7.20 dz. F-984 3 asst. 5.40 dz.

-612 3 asst. 4.80 dz. F-774 3 asst. 7.80 dz. F-687 3 asst. 2.70 dz. F-30 4 asst. 4.20 dz. F-858 3 asst. 5.40 dz. F-729 3 asst. 6.60 dz. F-917 3 asst. 6.00 dz.

TROPICAL BIRDS AND DOLPHIN ACCESSORIES

⑥

12"

11"

14½"

20"

A-406 (Plastic) 2/ast

A-121 (Plastic) 2/ast

A-506 (Planter) 30.00 dz/pc

E-433 (Planter) 48.00 dz/pc

A-643 (Plastic) 3/ast 15.00 dz/pc

A-100 (Plastic) 3/ast 6.00 dz/pc

A-405 (Plastic) 2/ast 10.20 dz/pc

10.20 dz/pc

15.00 dz/pc

5"

4"

C-800 10.80 dz/pc

H-38 (S/P) 12.00 dz/pr

H-137 (S/P) 12.00 dz/pr

A-192 2/ast 12.00 dz/pc

A-356 3/ast 7.80 dz/pc

A-571 (3/pc set) 24.00 dz/st

A-630 (2/pc set) 13.50 dz/st

7½"

9½"

8"

9½"

8"

LOVELY HANDCRAFTED MUSIC BOXES AND FIGURINES

7"

6½"

6½"

6½"

F-481 (Music Box) 2/ast 66.00 dz/pc

F-900 (Music box) 3/ast 60.00 dz/pc

F-901 (Music Box) 3/ast 60.00 dz/pc

F-902 (Music box) 3/ast 60.00 dz/pc

6"

5"

5"

F-490 (Music box) 3/ast 54.00 dz/pc

F-493 (Music box) 48.00 dz/pc

10"

Y-201 (Music box) 60.00 dz/pc

W-501 (Music box) 4/ast 39.00 dz/pc

F-445 (Electric lights) 2/ast 36.00 dz/pc

8"

8"

9"

Selections from 1974 Norcrest Fine Gifts and China catalog

H-1 18.00 dz/pr   H-7 18.00 dz/pr   H-9 18.00 dz/pr   H-14 15.00 dz/pr   H-15 15.00 dz/pr   H-18 18.00 dz/pr   H-21 18.00 dz/pr   H-22 18.00 dz/pr

H-33 15.00 dz/pr   H-38 12.00 dz/pr   H-39 12.00 dz/pr   H-59 15.00 dz/pr   H-61 9.00 dz/pr   H-62 9.00 dz/pr   H-65 12.00 dz/st   H-101 12.00 dz/pr

H-107 15.00 dz/pr   H-111 15.00 dz/pr   H-115 9.00 dz/pr   H-116 9.00 dz/pr   H-122 15.00 dz/pr   H-130 2/ast 9.00 dz/pr   H-132 15.00 dz/pr   H-133 9.00 dz/pr   H-137 15.00 dz/pr

H-138 9.00 dz/pr   H-148 12.00 dz/pr   H-149 12.00 dz/pr   H-144 12.00 dz/pr   H-151 12.00 dz/pr   H-156 12.00 dz/pr   H-157 12.00 dz/pr   H-158 12.00 dz/pr

H-159 3/ast 12.00 dz/pr   H-161 12.00 dz/pr   H-169 15.00 dz/pr   H-170 15.00 dz/pr   H-173 12.00 dz/pr   H-174 12.00 dz/pr   H-175 12.00 dz/pr   H-183 9.60 dz/pr

NORCREST OFFERS THE WIDEST VARIETY IN ORIGINAL DESIGN SALT AND PEPPER SETS

H-186 9.60 dz/pr   H-188 9.60 dz/pr   H-193 12.00 dz/pr   H-196 12.00 dz/pr   H-197 12.00 dz/pr   H-198 13.50 dz/pr   H-199 12.00 dz/pr   H-202 10.20 dz/pr

H-204 10.20 dz/pr   H-205 10.20 dz/pr   H-190 15.00 dz/pr   H-215 9.00 dz/pr   H-221 15.00 dz/pr   H-232 9.00 dz/pr   H-233 9.00 dz/pr

H-238 9.60 dz/pr   H-241 15.00 dz/st   H-242 12.00 dz/st   H-243 12.00 dz/st   H-250 9.00 dz/pr   H-254 12.00 dz/pr   H-258 10.20 dz/pr   H-260 12.00 dz/pr

H-261 15.00 dz/pr   H-264 15.00 dz/pr   H-269 15.00 dz/pr   H-270 15.00 dz/pr   H-271 15.00 dz/pr   H-273 15.00 dz/pr   H-274 12.00 dz/pr   H-275 9.00 dz/pr   H-277 12.00 dz/pr   H-279 12.00   H-285 15.00 dz/pr

H-289   H-290   H-291   H-292   H-293   H-294   H-295   H-297   H-298

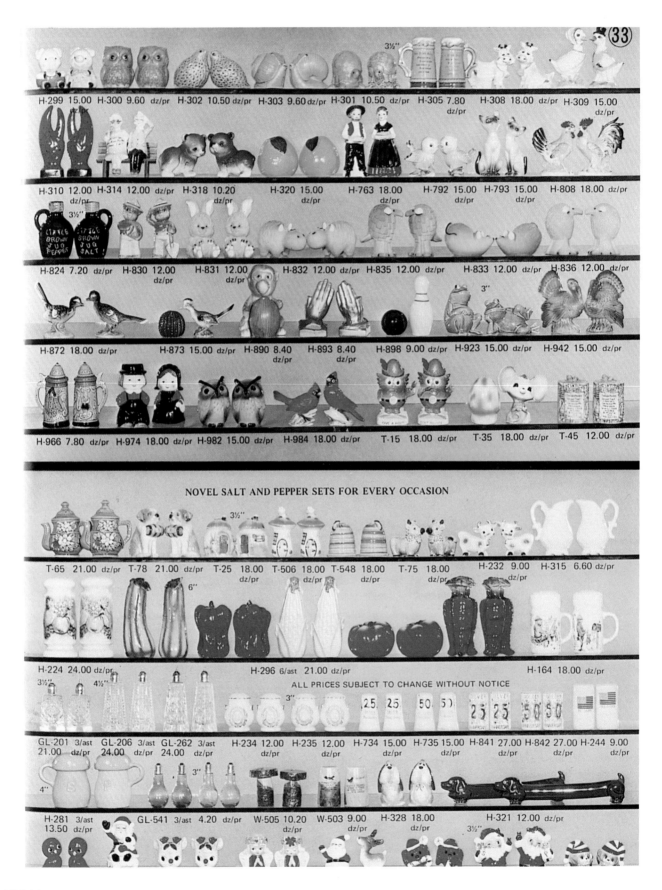

(33)

H-299 15.00 H-300 9.60 dz/pr H-302 10.50 dz/pr H-303 9.60 dz/pr H-301 10.50 dz/pr H-305 7.80 dz/pr H-308 18.00 dz/pr H-309 15.00 dz/pr

H-310 12.00 dz/pr H-314 12.00 dz/pr H-318 10.20 dz/pr H-320 15.00 dz/pr H-763 18.00 dz/pr H-792 15.00 dz/pr H-793 15.00 dz/pr H-808 18.00 dz/pr

H-824 7.20 dz/pr H-830 12.00 dz/pr H-831 12.00 dz/pr H-832 12.00 dz/pr H-835 12.00 dz/pr H-833 12.00 dz/pr H-836 12.00 dz/pr

H-872 18.00 dz/pr H-873 15.00 dz/pr H-890 8.40 dz/pr H-893 8.40 dz/pr H-898 9.00 dz/pr H-923 15.00 dz/pr H-942 15.00 dz/pr

H-966 7.80 dz/pr H-974 18.00 dz/pr H-982 15.00 dz/pr H-984 18.00 dz/pr T-15 18.00 dz/pr T-35 18.00 dz/pr T-45 12.00 dz/pr

NOVEL SALT AND PEPPER SETS FOR EVERY OCCASION

T-65 21.00 dz/pr T-78 21.00 dz/pr T-25 18.00 dz/pr T-506 18.00 dz/pr T-548 18.00 dz/pr T-75 18.00 dz/pr H-232 9.00 dz/pr H-315 6.60 dz/pr

H-224 24.00 dz/pr H-296 6/ast 21.00 dz/pr H-164 18.00 dz/pr

ALL PRICES SUBJECT TO CHANGE WITHOUT NOTICE

GL-201 3/ast 21.00 dz/pr GL-206 3/ast 24.00 dz/pr GL-262 3/ast 24.00 dz/pr H-234 12.00 dz/pr H-235 12.00 dz/pr H-734 15.00 dz/pr H-735 15.00 dz/pr H-841 27.00 dz/pr H-842 27.00 dz/pr H-244 9.00 dz/pr

H-281 3/ast 13.50 dz/pr GL-541 3/ast 4.20 dz/pr W-505 10.20 dz/pr W-503 9.00 dz/pr H-328 18.00 dz/pr H-321 12.00 dz/pr

J-264 (Musical Decanters)
2/ast 57.00 dz/pc

J-24
3/ast
9.00
dz/pc

J-227
7.80
dz/pc

NB-30 (Musical Decanters) 12/ast 42.00 dz/pc

J-294 2/ast
24.00 dz/pc

J-264 3ast
15.00 dz/pc

J-121 3/ast
12.00 dz/pc

J-381 4/ast
15.00 dz/pc

J-545 (Musical)
39.00 dz/pc

J-22 15.00
dz/pc

J-23 15.00
dz/st

J-122 15.00
dz/pc

J-299 15.00
dz/pc

NORCREST HAS STEINS FOR DECORATION AND FOR DRINKING

C-982 144.00 dz/pc

C-980 51.00 dz/pc

C-621
27.00
dz/pc

C-541
21.00
dz/pc

C-647 81.00 dz/pc

C-930 120.00 dz/pc

Selections from 1989 Norcrest Fine Gifts and China catalog

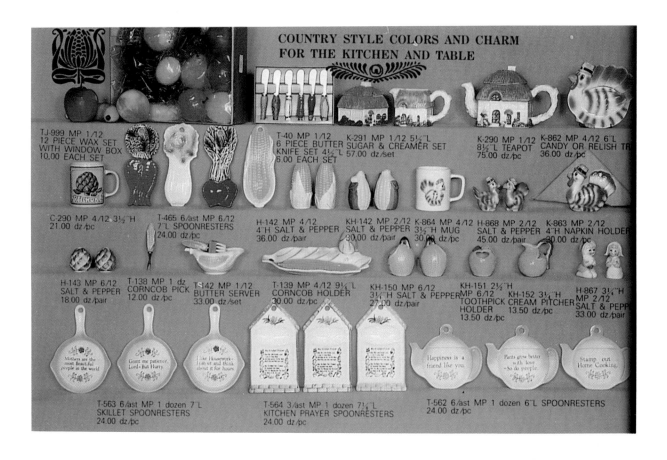

COUNTRY STYLE COLORS AND CHARM
FOR THE KITCHEN AND TABLE

TJ-999 MP 1/12
12 PIECE WAX SET
WITH WINDOW BOX
10.00 EACH SET

T-40 MP 1/12
6 PIECE BUTTER
KNIFE SET 4½"L
6.00 EACH SET

K-291 MP 1/12 5¼"L
SUGAR & CREAMER SET
57.00 /set

K-290 MP 1/12
8½"L TEAPOT
75.00 /pc

K-862 MP 4/12 6"L
CANDY OR RELISH TR
36.00 dz/pc

C-290 MP 4/12 3½"H
21.00 dz/pc

T-465 6/ast MP 6/12
7"L SPOONRESTERS
24.00 dz/pc

H-142 MP 4/12
4"H SALT & PEPPER
36.00 dz/pair

KH-142 MP 2/12
SALT & PEPPER
30.00 dz/pair

K-864 MP 4/12
3½"H MUG
30.00 dz/pc

H-868 MP 2/12
SALT & PEPPER
45.00 dz/pair

K-863 MP 2/12
4"H NAPKIN HOLDER
30.00 dz/pc

H-143 MP 6/12
SALT & PEPPER
18.00 dz/pair

T-138 MP 1 dz
CORNCOB PICK
12.00 dz/pc

T-142 MP 1/12
BUTTER SERVER
33.00 dz/set

T-139 MP 4/12 9¼"L
CORNCOB HOLDER
30.00 dz/pc

KH-150 MP 6/12
3¼"H SALT & PEPPER
27.00 dz/pair

KH-151 2½"H
MP 6/12
TOOTHPICK
HOLDER
13.50 dz/pc

KH-152 3½"H
CREAM PITCHER
13.50 dz/pc

H-867 3½"H
MP 2/12
SALT & PEPP
33.00 dz/pair

T-563 6/ast MP 1 dozen 7"L
SKILLET SPOONRESTERS
24.00 dz/pc

T-564 3/ast MP 1 dozen 7¼"L
KITCHEN PRAYER SPOONRESTERS
24.00 dz/pc

T-562 6/ast MP 1 dozen 6"L SPOONRESTERS
24.00 dz/pc

ROMANTIC BLUEBOY AND PINKY GIRL FIGURINES,
ELEGANT LADY FIGURINES AND MUSIC BOXES

62

F-398 2/ast MP 2/12 11¼"H
14.00 EACH PIECE

F-415 2/ast MP 2/12 8"H
60.00 dz/pc

F-390 MP 1/12 7½"H
9.00 EACH PIECE

F-945 3/ast MP 3/12 8½"H 10.00 EACH
MUSIC BOX: JEANNIE WITH LIGHT BRO

F-394 2/ast MP 2/12 5 3/4"H
20.00 EACH PIECE

F-913 MP 1/12 7"H 7.75 EACH PIECE
MUSIC BOX: RAINDROPS
ARE FALLING ON MY HEAD

F-404 4/ast MP 4/12 BONECHINA 7½"H 11.00 EACH

F-823 MP 1/12 6"H
MUSIC BOX:
LOVE STORY
12.50 EACH PIECE

F-927 MB MP 1/12 6"H
MUSIC BOX:
EASTER PARADE
10.00 EACH PIECE

F-928 MP 1/12
MBX: EASTER PARADE
10.00 EACH PIECE

F-880 MP 1/12
MBX: SOUND OF
MUSIC
8.00 EACH PIECE

F-881 MP 1/12
MBX: JEANNIE
LIGHT BROWN HAIR
8.00 EACH PIECE

F-915 2/ast MP 2/12 5"H
MUSIC BOX: TRUE LOVE
8.00 EACH PIECE

F-968
MBS
ME TE
10.00

Selections from 1989 Norcrest Fine Gifts and China catalog

CLASSIC "BLUE WILLOW" KITCHENWARE ACCESSORIES

BW-83
MP 1/12
CHURCHILL
SUGAR ONLY
5.75 EACH

BW-396 MP 1/12 10"L
SOUP TUREEN & LADLE SET
24.00 EACH SET

BW-902 MP 1/12 13"D
SERVING PLATTER
12.00 EACH PIECE

BW-80 MP 1/12 8"L
CHURCHILL POTTERY
MADE IN ENGLAND
20.00 EACH PIECE

BW-81 MP 1/12 3½"D
CHURCHILL POTTERY
MADE IN ENGLAND
CUP ONLY
2.00 EACH PIECE

BW-82 MP 1/12
CHURCHILL
SAUCER ONLY
1.50 EACH PC

BW-84 MP 1/12
CHURCHILL
CREAMER ONLY
4.24 EACH

BLUE WILLOW

BW-389 MP 1/12 11"L PLATTER
14.00 EACH PIECE
BW-386 MP 3/12 9 3/4"D
SERVING BOWL

BW-388 MP 1/12
11¼"D PLATTER
12.00 EACH PIECE

BW-85 MP 1/12
CHURCHILL
7"D PLATE
1.75 EACH PIECE

BW-86 MP 1/12
CHURCHILL POTTERY
8"D PLATE
2.25 EACH PIECE

BW-87 MP 1/12
CHURCHILL POTTERY
10¼"D PLATE
3.00 EACH PIECE

BW-91 MP 1/12
CHURCHILL POTTERY
12½"L PLATTER
9.00 EACH PIECE

BW-387 MP 6/12
6¼"D BOWL
36.00 dz/pc
CHURCHILL

BW-92 MP 1 dz
CHURCHILL
2½"H EGG CUP
13.50 dz/pc

BW-88 MP 1/12
CHURCHILL POTTERY
6"D BOWL

BW-89 MP 1/12
CHURCHILL POTTERY
8"D BOWL

BW-90 MP 1/12 9"D
CHURCHILL POTTERY

CLASSIC "BLUE WILLOW" TABLEWARE ACCESSORIES

BW-122 MP 2/12
7"H COFFEE POT
10.00 EACH PIECE

BW-120 MP 2/12
TEAPOT
00 EACH PIECE

BW-121 MP 1 dozen
5½" EGGSHELL PORCELAIN
CUP WITH GEISHA LADY
45.00 dz/pc

BW-129 MP 1/12
6"H GINGER JAR
8.00 EACH PIECE

BW-131 MP 6/12
6"H VASE
5.50 EACH PIECE

BW-173 MP 1/12
8½"L TEAPOT
12.00 EACH PIECE

BW-170 MP 1/12
6"H TEAPOT
12.00 EACH PIECE

BW-128 MP 1 dz
5"D RICE BOWL
13.50 dz/pc

BW-126 MP 3 dz
PICKLE DISH
12.00 dz/pc

BW-133 MP 1 dz
4½"D A/D C & S
36.00 dz/pc

BW-123 MP 1/12
SUGAR & CREAMER
7.00 EACH SET

BW-132
MP 1 dz 3½"H MUG
VASE 30.00 dz/pc

BW-174 MP 6/12

BW-171 MP 1/12
SUGAR & CREAMER
9.00 EACH SET

BW-130 3½"H
MP 6/12
GINGER JAR
39.00 dz/pc

BLUE WILLOW

BW-182 MP 6/12
7"D RICE BOWL
90.00 dz/pc

BW-181 MP 1 dz
4½"D RICE BOWL
27.00 dz/pc

BW-150 MP 3/12
10½"D PLATE
90.00 dz/pc

BW-177 MP 1 dozen
5"D 2 PIECE ASHTRAY SET
8.50 EACH SET

BW-183 MP 1 dozen
2¼"D TEA CUP
24.00 dz/pc

BW-176 MP 4/12 12½"L PLATTER
8.50 EACH PIECE

BW-175 MP 1/12
7"L BUTTERDISH
8.00 EACH PIECE

BW-185 MP 1 dozen
5"L SOUP SPOON
9.00 dz/pc

BW-180 MP 1 dozen
1½"H PICK HOLDER
21.00 dz/pc

BW-178 MP 1/12 4"H
3 POTS WITH SAUCERS SET

228

Selections from 1993 – 94 Norcrest Fine Gifts and China catalog

NOVEL TEAPOTS & PORCELAIN TEAPOTS

KT-220 "TEA FOR TWO"
TEAPOT & 2 MUGS
6"LG MIN 1 SET
10.00 SET

21

K-260 PITCHER
8 1/3"H MIN 1 PC
18.00 EACH

TK-266 TEAPOT
8"LG MIN 1 PC
9.50 EACH

KL-100 TEAPOT
7"H MIN 1 PC
9.00 EACH

KL-212 TEAPOT
8"H MIN 1 PC
14.00 EACH

PHW-831   SUG+CRM
3 3/4"DR M=1 SET
9.50 SET

K-231 TEAPOT 7"LG
M=1 PC> 7.00 EACH

K-232 TEAPOT
7"LG ON 1 PC
7.00 EACH

K-235 TEAPOT
& CUP MIN 1 PC
13.00 EACH

K-236 TEAPOT
8 1/2"LG MIN 1 PC
13.00 EACH

PHW-830   TEAPOT
7 3/4"LG M=1 PC
11.00 EACH

TK-261 TEAPOT
8 1/2" LONG
MIN 1 PC
10.00 EACH

*TK-262 TEAPOT
8 1/2" LONG
MIN 1 PC
10.00 EACH

TK-263 TEAPOT
9"LG MIN 1 PC
10.00 EACH

TK-264 TEAPOT
8 1/2" LONG
MIN 1 PC
10.00 EACH

*TK-265 TEAPOT
MIN 1 PIECE
10.00 EACH

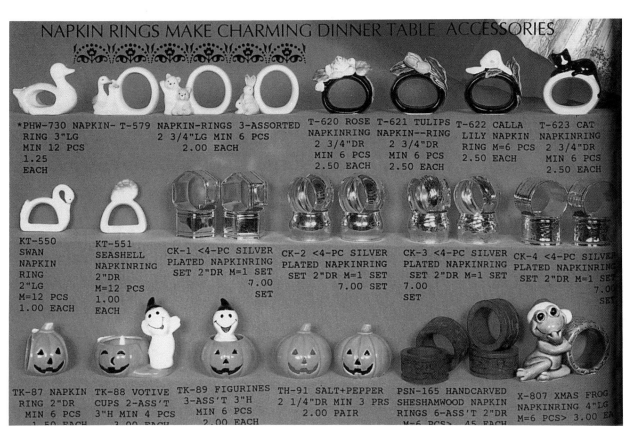

NAPKIN RINGS MAKE CHARMING DINNER TABLE ACCESSORIES

*PHW-730 NAPKIN-
RING 3"LG
MIN 12 PCS
1.25
EACH

T-579 NAPKIN-RINGS 3-ASSORTED
2 3/4"LG MIN 6 PCS
2.00 EACH

T-620 ROSE
NAPKINRING
2 3/4"DR
MIN 6 PCS
2.50 EACH

T-621 TULIPS
NAPKIN--RING
2 3/4"DR
MIN 6 PCS
2.50 EACH

T-622 CALLA
LILY NAPKIN
RING M=6 PCS
2.50 EACH

T-623 CAT
NAPKINRING
2 3/4"DR
MIN 6 PCS
2.50 EACH

KT-550
SWAN
NAPKIN
RING
2"LG
M=12 PCS
1.00 EACH

KT-551
SEASHELL
NAPKINRING
2"DR
M=12 PCS
1.00
EACH

CK-1 <4-PC SILVER
PLATED NAPKINRING
SET 2"DR M=1 SET
7.00
SET

CK-2 <4-PC SILVER
PLATED NAPKINRING
SET 2"DR M=1 SET
7.00 SET

CK-3 <4-PC SILVER
PLATED NAPKINRING
SET 2"DR M=1 SET
7.00
SET

CK-4 <4-PC SILVER
PLATED NAPKINRING
SET 2"DR M=1 SET
7.00
SET

TK-87 NAPKIN
RING 2"DR
MIN 6 PCS
1.50 EACH

TK-88 VOTIVE
CUPS 2-ASS'T
3"H MIN 4 PCS
2.00 EACH

TK-89 FIGURINES
3-ASS'T 3"H
MIN 6 PCS
2.00 EACH

TH-91 SALT+PEPPER
2 1/4"DR MIN 3 PRS
2.00 PAIR

PSN-165 HANDCARVED
SHESHAMWOOD NAPKIN
RINGS 6-ASS'T 2"DR
M=6 PCS> .45 EACH

X-807 XMAS FROG
NAPKINRING 4"LG
M=6 PCS> 3.00 EA

Selections from 1993 – 94 Norcrest Fine Gifts and China catalog

46

ELECTRIC HOUSE LIGHTS & HOUSE ORNAMENTS

TJ-590 ELECTRIC CORD LIGHT "THE TRAIN STATION" 6 1/2"LG MIN 1 PC> 15.00 EACH

TJ-591 ELECTRIC CORD LIGHT "COUNTRRY STORE" 6 1/2"LG MIN 1 PC 15.00 EACH

TJ-592 ELECTRIC CORD LIGHT "COUNTRY INN" 6 1/2'LG MIN 1 PC> 15.00 EACH

TJ-593 ELECTRIC CORD LIGHT "COUNTRY CHURCH" 6 1/2" LONG MIN 1 PC 15.00 EACH

HK-650 OLDTYME HOUSE ORNAMENTS 6-ASSORTED 3 1/2" LONG MIN 6 PCS> 3.25 EACH

CH-3 OLDE ENGLISH BREWERY ORNAMENT 4 1/2"H MIN 1 PC> 8.00 EACH

CH-1 <4-PIECE OLDE ENGLISH COTTAGE ORNAMENT SET 2 1/2"LG MIN 1 SET 7.50 SET

CH-2 <3-PIECE OLDE ENGLISH COTTAGE ORNAMENT SET 3"LG MIN 1 SET 7.50 SET

COTTAGES & CASTLES GIFTWARE IDEAS

K-290 COTTAGE TEAPOT 8 1/2"LG MIN 1 PC 9.50 EACH

TF-607 FIGURINES 3-ASS'T 6" HIGH MIN 3 PCS 3.00 EACH

PP-992 CACHE POT 5 1/2"DR & HIGH MINIMUM 4 PIECES 3.00 EACH

#4823 "OLDE ENGLISH VILLAGES" ENGLISH BONE CHINA PLATES 4-ASSORTED 8"DR MIN 4 PCS 12.00 EACH

K-291 COTTAGE SUGAR & CREAMER SET 5 1/2"LG MIN 1 SET 7.00 SET

#4855 "ENGLISH COTTAGES" ENGLISH BONE CHINA MUGS 3-ASSORTED MIN 6 PCS 11.00 EACH

#4864 "ENGLISH FARMS" ENGLISH BONE CHINA MUGS 4-ASSORTED MIN 4 PCS 10.00 EACH

CH-104 ENGLISH HOUSE ORNAMENT 4 1/4"H MIN 1 PC 5.00 EACH

CH-3 ENGLISH BREWERY ORNAMENT 4 1/2"H MIN 1 PC 8.00 EACH

CH-5 ENGLISH HOUSE ORNAMENT 3 1/2"H MIN 1 PIECE 4.75 EACH

CH-6 ENGLISH HOUSE ORNAMENT MIN 1 PC 2 3/4"H> 8.00 EACH

CH-100 OLD CASTLE ORNAMENT MIN 1 PC 10.00 EACH

CH-101 OLD CASTLE ORNAMENT MIN 1 PC 7.00 EACH

ABOUT THE AUTHOR

Carole Bess White is the author of two other Collector Books, *The Collector's Guide to Made in Japan Ceramics, Volumes 1 and 2*. She has been a serious collector of Made in Japan since 1981. She is also a collector in many other categories, including Depression Glass, and a 1920s and '30s movie fan. For a number of years she was also a potter, producing wheel-thrown stoneware and raku vessels.

She started the *Made in Japan Info Letter*, a national newsletter on the subject of Made in Japan, and is a member of the Noritake Society, National Cambridge Collectors, Inc., the Tiffin Glass Collectors Club, and a lifetime member of Portland's Rain of Glass. Carole has worked full-time in newspaper entertainment advertising for more than 25 years. Research on Made in Japan is a major interest of Carole's, and she plans to continue those studies.

Les White, Ed.D., has spent many years working with photography and computers. At present he is middle school principal and information technology coordinator for an area K-12 school. Les collects nothing but computers! The Whites reside in Portland, Oregon.

BIBLIOGRAPHY

Cushing, Richard, "The Japanese Patent Numbering System." Des Moines, Iowa: Article, *Antique and Collectors Reproduction News,* May 1997.

Katz-Marks, Mariann, *The Collector's Encyclopedia of Majolica*. Paducah, Ky: Collector Books, 1992.

Noritake, *History of the Materials Development and Chronology of the Backstamps,* Noritake Company Ltd., May 1997.

Van Patten, Joan, *The Collector's Encyclopedia of Noritake.* Paducah, Ky: Collector Books, 1984.

Van Patten, Joan, *The Collector's Encyclopedia of Noritake, Second Series.* Paducah, Ky: Collector Books, 1994.

INDEX